FOOTBALL'S

44

STACK DEFENSE

TOM SIMONTON

MacGregor Sports Education

Waukesha, Wisconsin

Library of Congress Cataloging-in-Publication Data

Simonton, Tom
    Football's 44 stack defense / Tom Simonton.
        p.   cm.
    ISBN 0-941175-35-9
    1. Football--Defense.   I. Title.   II. Title: Football's forty
  -four stack defense.
  GV951.18.S56   1989
  796.332'2--dc20   89-32553
                                                                           CIP

ISBN 0-941175-35-9

Printed in the United States of America

Dedicated to
Lyn, Mike, David, and Steve, who are always there,
win or lose.

Introducing the
44 Stack Defense

The 44 Stack defense, which we first introduced twenty years ago, continues to present us with what we consider to be the most flexible defense in existence. It was designed to create doubt and confusion in blocking assignments. It does that. It was designed to provide an attacking defense that challenges the offense on each play. It does that. It was designed to allow smaller, quicker players to play anywhere on our defense, even at defensive tackle. They can. It was designed to present maximum pass coverage and to pressure the opponent's running game. It has succeeded.

Success has followed the defense. We've used it at three different schools and each has become a winner. The defense has led us to winning seasons, post-season playoffs, and city championships. Our players love to play the defense and become closely identified with it.

This book describes everything needed to put the 44 Stack defense into operation, from basic philosophy to basic alignment. It describes all stunts—for this is indeed a stunting defense—and introduces two special added features, the Rover and the 45 Adjustment, which we added to the defense in recent years.

We feel your players will love the challenge of a blitzing, attacking defense. And you as a coach will find it the most adjustable defense imaginable. You'll be able to place your players where you want them with simple stunt calls. We hope the material in this book will enlighten and challenge your thinking on defense.

Tom Simonton

Contents

1

The Goals and Basic Alignment of the 44 Stack

Regardless of the type of defense you use, you must have a strong belief in the ability of that defense to control your opponent's offense, week by week. This belief in the value of your defense must be strong enough for you to transfer this confidence to the players who will actually execute the defense. This confidence comes through a complete understanding of the goals and advantages, as well as the finer points of the defense. Once the players and coaches alike understand the basic goals of the defense and can see the overall picture of what is to be accomplished, they can more easily accept the details of playing the defense.

MAJOR GOALS OF THE 44 STACK

Following are the three major goals of the 44 Stack defense.

1. Stop the long touchdown run or pass. We want to take away the easy touchdown by making our opponents have to drive slowly, yard-by-yard, before crossing our goal line. Many high school football teams are scored on more by the sudden long run or pass than by the constant down-the-field drive. If we can make our opponents have to drive slowly towards our goal line, there is a good chance that a fumble, a penalty, or their own blocking failure against our 44 Stack will force them to have to turn the ball over to us.

We feel we can take away the long run or pass by utilizing three safety men, each of whom has the responsibility of playing a deep one-third of the field. Each man is given one major assignment—"Let no offensive player get behind you." Unlike many defenses, we do not require our safety men to rotate as the play develops. Before the development of the 44 Stack, we had used a rotating type secondary, but found it rotating too slowly at times and committing too quickly at other times. This tended to create holes in our deep defensive positions. Therefore, our first decision in developing the 44 Stack was to establish a solid three-deep, no-rotation secondary to prevent the long run or pass. By doing this we cut to one-sixth the number of long plays against our defense over what it had been the previous season. And when we did give up the long play we found that it was rarely the fault of the defensive positioning of our safety men, but rather that our defender was physically not fast enough or tall enough to stay with his opponent.

2. Force the offense to do what it doesn't want to do. We try to take away the favorite plays of the offense by positioning our players to stop their "bread and butter" plays. In other words, if we are playing a team that favors the passing game, we position our defense to take away the passing game and force the offense to run the ball. If the opponents like to run, we try to force them to pass. If the offense likes to run wide, we use stunts to stop the wide plays and make the offense run up the middle. Against a team that has big, slow backs and heavy linemen we will stunt inside and try to force the backs outside. If the opponent has a strong trapping offense, the 44 Stack can stunt in such a manner as to make the trap play ineffective.

3. Confuse the blocking assignments of the offensive linemen. The design of the 44 Stack defense enables any of the eleven defensive players to stunt across the line of scrimmage into the offensive backfield. When the defensive team uses a well-known defense, such as the Oklahoma 5–4 or the wide-tackle 6, the offensive team has a reasonably sure idea of where the defenders will be at the snap of the ball. This is not true of the 44 Stack defense, as you will see in Chapter 3. Unless the high school lineman is extremely well coached, he will find it most difficult to consistently block the correct defender and to block him properly. When we have created doubt in the mind of the offensive blocker about which defender to block, we feel we have gone a long way towards making sure he will not make a good block.

ADVANTAGES OF USING THE 44 STACK DEFENSE

1. Opponents must prepare differently for it. Because of its alignment, the 44 Stack will look different to the offense. It presents the offensive coach with the problem of devising and teaching a new set of blocking assignments in an attempt to overcome the shifting and stunting of the 44 Stack defense. Without a great deal of planning and concentration the offense will have little chance of blocking successfully against the defense. The opponents will have to spend a good part of their practice sessions preparing for the 44 Stack, thereby neglecting other important areas of preparation.

2. *Utilization of four linebackers is the key to its success.* We feel that linebackers, with freedom to move laterally, are the key to any successful defense. The 44 Stack is designed with four linebackers, whereas most other defenses have two or sometimes three. These four linebackers are usually hidden behind front linemen, making them hard to find and presenting the problem of which way they will be moving when the ball is snapped. These linebackers have a variety of moves they can make. They can play soft or they can stunt across the line of scrimmage. They sometimes key the ball, being ready to move laterally right or left. Often, before the snap, a linebacker will move head-on an uncovered offensive lineman, forcing the offensive lineman to plan to block him, only to have the linebacker move back out of sight. And once the ball is in play the four linebackers have freedom of movement to pursue.

3. *44 Stack defense is flexible.* We can attack the offense by using one or a combination of the stunts described in Chapter 3. These stunts are designed to place defensive personnel at any area where the offensive team is giving us trouble. Or we can utilize as many as seven players on pass defense when necessary. Whether you wish your defense to pressure the offense, or to play the loose waiting type defense, the 44 Stack can provide either.

4. *Small players can be used in the 44 Stack defense.* One of the main reasons we designed the 44 Stack defense as we did was because of the lack of large players, both in the line and at the linebacker positions. In the 44 Stack defense, smaller players are seldom called on to battle head-on with opponents much larger than themselves. Because of the movement of the defensive players as the ball is snapped, the offensive linemen rarely get a clear, head-on meeting with the smaller defensive players. However, if your squad is blessed with larger defensive players, you may choose to let your linemen meet head-on and engage in man-to-man battle with the opponent. This method of play can also be accomplished with the 44 Stack.

5. *The offense will be thrown for losses several times during the course of the game.* By utilizing the stunts of the 44 Stack effectively, we have never failed to catch an opposing back for a loss of yardage at least once during the course of a game. In fact, on more than one occasion, we have had the same linebacker break through on three consecutive plays to throw the offensive back for a loss. However, as you

can imagine, it usually takes only one of these breakthroughs to place the offense in a long yardage situation.

6. Players can interchange within their defensive positions. 44 Stack players are assigned to one of three groups of positions—front linemen, linebackers, or safety men. All front linemen will be taught the same stance, stunts, and basic movements. Because of this, the best four linemen can be starters, and the next best lineman used as a substitute for any of the four, regardless of where on the line of scrimmage they were playing. The same is true of the linebackers and safety men. There is another advantage to being able to interchange players within their group. Let's say that the best linebacker on the defensive team was playing on the extreme left side of the defense, and that the offensive team was running effectively to the right side of the defense. The linebacker could easily swap over to the right side with no change in position techniques or assignments to learn. Or the same linebacker could move to an inside linebacker position with equal ease. Along the same idea, the best of the four front linemen could be moved anywhere along the front line in order to match him up with a particularly good offensive player. There would be no change in technique or style of play to learn. This ease in interchanging players is, we feel, one of the real strong points of the 44 Stack.

7. Defensive players enjoy playing the defense. This was one of the first things we noticed as we were developing the 44 Stack. We found our players beginning to take a special interest in defense because they felt they had a defense that other teams didn't have. Our players developed a great confidence and pride in the ability of the defense. They felt they couldn't be scored on, and often they were right!

DEFENSIVE POSITIONS OF THE 44 STACK

The 44 Stack defense consists of three waves of defenders: the front four, the four linebackers, and the three safety men.

1. Front four. The front four is made up of four linemen who play on the line of scrimmage. They are actually defensive ends and defensive tackles. The ends will line up head-on the offensive ends. The tackles will line up head-on the offensive guards (Figure 1-1).

All front four linemen should use a four-point stance. Since the front four players are often called on to move laterally and at angles, as well as straight ahead, we do not allow them to use a four-point stance where great pressure is put on the hands. We feel that too much pressure on the hands commits the lineman to going in a general straight-ahead pattern.

To get in the proper stance, each front four lineman should first stand upright with each foot about six inches wider than the shoulder. He should then bend the knees and lean forward, placing his hands gently on

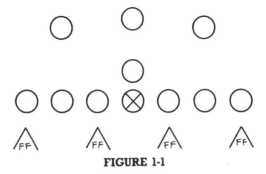

FIGURE 1-1

the ground about fifteen inches in front of him. The lineman should be balanced on his legs and should feel very little pressure on his hands. Some linemen even touch the ground with only their fingertips. From this stance each front four player should feel that he has more freedom to move in any direction than if he was leaning forward heavily on his hands.

Each of the front four players should locate about 15 to 18 inches off the line of scrimmage, except on extremely short yardage situations when it may be necessary to get slightly closer.

Care should be taken to observe the stance and positioning of each front four man at regular intervals during the season. This will insure that the lineman is following the fundamentals of stance and positioning which will allow him proper movement in any direction. You should also make sure the front four player is not getting too near the line of scrimmage where the offensive player can get to him before he is able to move.

One of the real keys to the success of the 44 Stack is the fact that our ends are lined up head-on the offensive ends instead of inside or outside of them. If the defensive end was inside, the offensive end could easily block him in. If outside, the offensive end would have no trouble riding him out, opening the off-tackle hole. Having the defensive end locate head-on the offensive end, and then having him move right or left or blast straight ahead on the snap of the ball, creates a real problem for the blocker. The offensive end cannot predetermine how he is going to block the defensive end; therefore, he usually has trouble making a successful block.

2. Linebackers. The second line of defense consists of four linebackers. Each of the four linebackers lines up or "stacks" directly behind a front four man, giving the name *44 Stack* to our defense (Figure 1-2).

All four linebackers should use the two-point, upright stance, with the knees slightly bent. They should line up with both feet parallel and about shoulder width apart. Weight should be evenly distributed on both feet allowing the linebacker to move quickly in any direction.

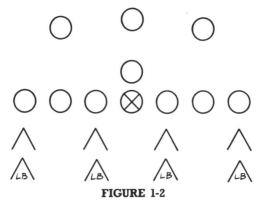

FIGURE 1-2

The linebacker should not crowd the front four man in front of him, but should be able to touch the back of his belt. Never allow the linebacker to turn his body at an angle away from the line of scrimmage, as this might prevent him from making quick lateral movement in any direction. It could also tip off the direction of a stunt if that linebacker happens to be involved in one.

3. Safety men. The third line of defense is handled by three safety men. We call them all "safety men" instead of calling the middle defender a "safety" and the other two defenders "halfbacks."

The left and right safety men normally line up three yards outside a normally positioned offensive end, and from seven to nine yards deep (Figure 1-3). This depth will vary slightly according to down, distance, and field position.

The outside foot of the left and right safety men should be back and the defenders should be facing at a slight angle to the outside. Their first

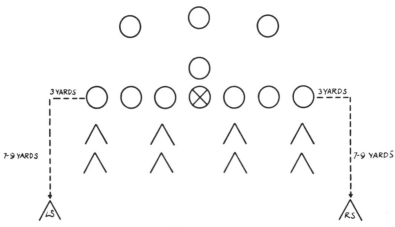

FIGURE 1-3

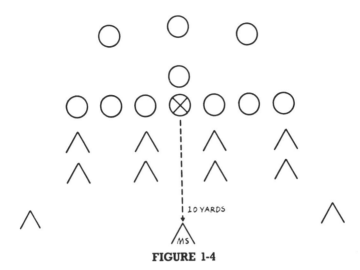

FIGURE 1-4

step should be back and to the outside, as this is a constant reminder of their deep one-third of the field pass defense responsibilities.

The middle safety is the deepest man in the defense. He normally aligns himself with the offensive center and about ten yards deep (Figure 1-4). As with the left and right safety men this depth will vary according to down, distance, and field position.

He has a balanced stance, favoring neither side until he has determined the nature of the play. His first step should be back, reminding him of his deep one-third pass defense responsibility.

The middle safety must learn to key the offensive guards to help determine a pass or a run, and he most certainly should never let an offensive player get behind him.

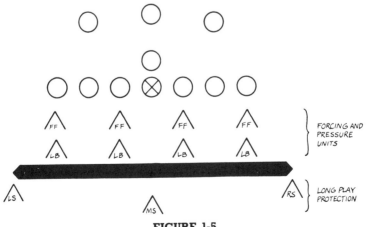

FIGURE 1-5

In *summary,* the strategy of the 44 Stack is to use the front four and linebackers as a forcing body to attack and pressure the offense at its strongest areas, and to stunt often, causing a general confusion in blocking assignments. This is done while at the same time keeping three safety men deep to protect against the long run or pass (Figure 1-5).

2

Placing Personnel
in the 44 Stack

One of the main duties of any coach is the placement of his personnel. You should spend as much time studying your personnel as you do working with the type and style of your defense or offense. Too often coaches use a player at a certain position just because the boy played that position on other teams at a younger age. Sometimes a boy reports for practice, tells the coach he wants to play defensive end, and here he remains until he graduates, with the coach never considering other possibilities. Maybe the boy is a good defensive end, but how is the coach sure that he isn't a great linebacker or safety man.

Each coach, regardless of what defensive alignment he uses, should have methods of testing the abilities of each player to establish what positions he can play and, of those positions, which one he is best suited for. Often the coach's needs will help solve the problem. Let's say that the coach has an excellent defensive end returning from last season's team. He also has two young defensive ends who can handle the job, but aren't versatile or experienced enough to play elsewhere. The good, experienced defensive end could be shifted to another position such as linebacker to help fill in for a possible weakness there.

We like to use early practice to experiment with different players at different positions. This experimenting serves three purposes:

1. We may find that we have been playing a boy "out of position" and that he is actually better suited for another position in our defense.

2. This experimenting gives our players a chance to get familiar with other defensive positions which they might have to play during the course of the season.

3. This shifting around of positions tends to familiarize the players with the "total picture" of what the defensive team is trying to do.

WHAT TO LOOK FOR IN DEFENSIVE PLAYERS

The defensive player must be ready for all situations—the power play, the quick pitch outside, the screen pass, the draw, the long pass, the reverse, or the trap. He must rely on four qualities in order to be a good defensive player. These qualities are *reaction, emotion, speed,* and *aggressiveness.* We do not worry a great deal about size when considering qualities for a good 44 Stack defensive player. Of course, if big players with the four qualities of reaction, emotion, speed, and aggressiveness are available, you are indeed fortunate. However, the 44 Stack defense doesn't require great size.

By *reaction* we mean players who can follow what is happening on the offensive side of the line of scrimmage and move into position to make the tackle. We want players who can move laterally quickly and who can react to a block. We want players who can get up after being blocked or knocked down, and still help make the tackle. When we have this, we have the type of reaction that can help us play good defense.

Small players who have good reaction can fit well into the 44 Stack defense. It does not take a physically large boy to be able to tackle the average high school back. If the boy can react and get into a good position to tackle, the defense will be in good shape.

We like our defense to have players who are *emotional.* This does not mean that we want eleven players to take the field at game time keyed so high that they will make mistakes and not be able to perform to their capacity. But it does mean that we want players who care enough about their team, their school, and their community to play with every bit of desire and ability that they possess.

Speed is different from reaction. Whereas, reaction can take place in a small 5- to 10-yard area, speed is used from sideline to sideline and from goal line to goal line. The 44 Stack defense needs as much speed as you can get into the lineup. This speed is needed to enable the players to pursue and to execute the stunts of the defense.

There is no substitute for speed. It is a great equalizer. If a defensive player gets faked or pulled out of position, speed can make up for it. If an offensive back gets free of the line of scrimmage, speed enables the defense to catch him.

By speed, we are not necessarily speaking of the 9.8 sprinters that few squads are blessed with. If you have several boys of 10.5 or 10.6 speed on the 100-yard dash, you should be able to place these men at certain positions where their speed can be used most effectively to control the offense.

Probably the most important quality to look for in a defensive player is *aggressiveness*. Reaction, speed, and emotion will do little good if a defensive player will not "hit" when he gets the opportunity.

We do feel that the way football is played today and with the large number of "specialists" on the squads, that there is a place on the team for the boy who just naturally is not overly aggressive. This type of player could become a punter, a kick-off or extra point specialist, or perhaps a flanker or split end. We feel this is good, for it gives all types of boys the opportunity to be a part of the game of football. However, all defensive players must be aggressive if the defense is to survive week after week. Aggressiveness is natural to some boys. You should seek these naturally aggressive boys when looking for defensive players.

A defensive team is fortunate if it contains several players with all four qualities of speed, reaction, emotion, and aggressiveness.

After we have found players with these four qualities, we are ready to place them in their proper positions. It is not our intention to make any position sound as though only superior football players can play the position. You should simply select the players who best fit the description of the type of player needed for each position.

Front Four

1. Defensive ends. Of the front four men available, the two defensive ends should be the best athletes. These players do not have to be extremely large. The main requirements are toughness and agility. The toughness is necessary to help control the off-tackle area. The agility is necessary to help play the outside on end sweeps and the like, when called on to do so.

We take the best of the two defensive ends and place him on the left side of our defense. This is because most teams are strongest running to their right, which is to our *left*. We want our best defensive end stationed where the offensive team is most likely to try to go.

The defensive ends should be strong tacklers. They should also take pride in rushing the passer and have enough movement to keep the passer from running around them for long gains. They must learn to use the forearm lift and hand shiver. Since the defensive ends stunt often, they should work to increase their quickness in getting across the line of scrimmage.

2. Defensive tackles. The largest players on the front four usually are placed at defensive tackle. Their job is basically to control the area inside the offensive tackles (with help from the inside linebackers). Since they generally do not have the responsibility of covering wide areas, speed is not quite as necessary here as at defensive end. However, remember that the defensive tackles will stunt often and that some speed is required. You should rarely sacrifice speed for size just for the sake of having "a couple of 200-pound players" in the lineup.

If larger, slower players must be in the lineup, then defensive tackle is where they should play. Since they will constantly be blocked by offensive guards and the center, some strength is required.

As with the defensive ends, the tackles should learn to use the forearm lift and hand shiver. They should work hard on rushing the passer and meeting the power play up the middle. Considerable time should also be spent on learning to read and play the trap.

Linebackers

1. Outside linebackers. This position demands two of the squad's best athletes. They should be dedicated players for they will be called on to learn to react to a pass or run by reading the keys of the offensive team. They do not have to be large, but must be strong enough to meet an end sweep effectively. At times they will play man-to-man pass defense, so some speed is required. The outside linebacker will have to make adjustments to some offensive formations and should be alert enough to realize when and how these adjustments should be made. And, of course, as with all 44 Stack players, the outside linebackers will be called on to execute stunts, so the ability to move quickly is very important.

2. Inside linebackers. An inside linebacker needs to be strong enough to help stop the running-play inside tackle and also needs to be agile enough to cover the middle area when playing zone pass defense. The inside linebacker isn't required to be quite as fast as an outside linebacker, but he should have good range. Since their normal position places them towards the inside of the offensive activity, the inside linebackers will have ample opportunity to be in on tackles from sideline to sideline.

Safety Men

1. Left and right safeties. The main requirement for the left and right safeties is speed. We like to use tall boys here, when they are available, for their pass defense ability. Basketball players on the football squad often make good safety prospects as they are already skilled in going after the ball and are usually fairly tall. Since these safety men must determine whether the play is a pass or run as quickly as possible, they should receive frequent practice on keying the offensive ends and backs. They should be able to play a wide flanker or split end man-to-man successfully.

Since plays coming their way are often near the sidelines, the left and right safeties must learn the sideline tackle and how to make the sideline work for them and serve as a "twelfth man." They should be sure, if not brutal, tacklers, for a missed tackle in open field can mean six points for the offense. These men must be disciplined to play the pass first and the run second, and at no time let an offensive end or back get behind them.

2. Middle safety. Since the middle safety is the last man between the offense and the goal line, he should be chosen with extreme care. He should be the most dependable tackler of the three safety men. He should learn to "read the play" quickly, and play pass defense first and play the run second. The middle safety is the "center fielder" for the entire defense and should be alert to the every move of the offense. He must be among the first to recognize the offensive formation and call the information out to his teammates. He should always point out flankers and split ends to the left and right safety men, so that no offensive player will ever fail to be noticed.

Here is a quick review to help in the placement of personnel:

1. Get as much speed in the lineup as possible.

2. Look for aggressive players who can react well and are willing to get themselves emotionally ready to play football.

3. Place the most agile of the front four players on the outside of the front four.

4. Place the larger and slower front four players at the two inside positions.

5. Two of the best athletes on the squad should be placed at the outside linebacker positions.

6. Inside linebackers should be able to stunt quickly across the line of scrimmage and should be good tacklers.

7. Speed is the key in selecting safety men.

BALANCING THE 44 STACK

After you have determined your best front four players, four linebackers, and three safety men, you should give considerable thought to exactly where each man fits in the total defense. A careful evaluation of your starting eleven players will show areas of potential strengths and weaknesses in the defensive lineup. You should think carefully about placing the proper balance of speed, strength, size, and experience throughout the defensive team. For instance, it is not desirable for all the size and strength to be placed on one side of the defense, leaving the other side physically weak. Likewise, all the experienced players should be spread evenly throughout the defense, leaving no area such as the middle or one side to the younger or unproved players.

If a potentially weak front four man is in the lineup, he should be backed by one of the strongest, most experienced linebackers. A large, slow front four man can be paired with a fast linebacker who can react quickly and cover for the lack of movement of the front four man. A good front four player can control his area in such a manner that he can keep a linebacker with less talent out of trouble. A tall, experienced middle safety can provide both height and leadership for two smaller and less experienced left and right safeties, who may be playing varsity football for the first time.

After all eleven starters have been placed in the defense, you should once again take a critical look at the overall alignment of your personnel. You may ask yourself these questions: "If I was the coach of the offensive team, what would I try to do against this alignment of personnel? Where are they the weakest in personnel? Where are their strong areas as far as personnel is concerned? What areas look slow? What areas should we avoid running toward?"

After all is said and done, the offense is playing against *people*, not chalk marks on the blackboard, and a thorough examination of the placement of personnel often can mean the difference between victory and defeat.

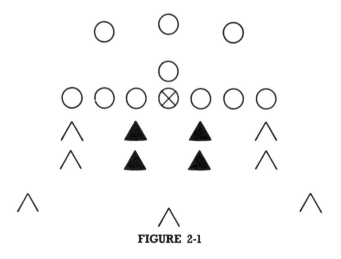

FIGURE 2-1

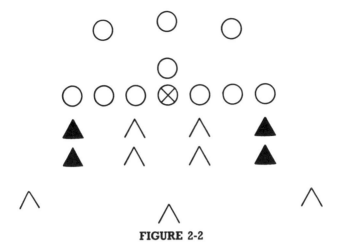

FIGURE 2-2

We spend countless hours during the off-season, not to mention the practice time leading up to the opening game, making absolutely sure that every possible player arrangement has been studied to insure the proper positioning of our 44 Stack players.

There is one exception to the plan of properly balancing the defense that should be brought to your attention. Occasionally, the defensive team will face an offensive team that has only one strength. Such a team, because of personnel, may be good at running inside tackle, but because of slow backfield personnel is absolutely no threat outside. You know that to stop their offense the defense must stop their inside attack, but you also know that the defense has little worry if the offense tries to get outside. In this case, the two best front four men and the two best linebackers may be moved to the inside positions of the defense (Figure 2-1). This defensive move should stop the inside attack of the offense, thereby taking away the thing they do best.

If the opposing team can run wide, but is no threat up the middle, the two best front four men and the two finest linebackers can be moved outside (Figure 2-2) in an effort to force the offense to run inside.

3

Setting Up the
44 Stack Numbering
System and Stunts

The strength of the 44 Stack defense is in its stunting and in its ease in calling a variety of stunts simply. This stunting must be done aggressively and forcefully, yet it must be tempered with adequate measures to contain the offense and prevent the long touchdown play. To use the 44 Stack and not stunt is like using only one offensive play during an entire game. The design of the 44 Stack enables it to cover as many areas as any other defense, yet the method of coverage is concealed from the offense until the snap. Although stunts other than the thirteen stunts included here can be devised, these thirteen are adequate to cover any situation and win, if they are taught and executed properly.

NUMBERING THE UNITS

Each of the four stack units in the 44 Stack defense is numbered. The left outside front four man and the left outside linebacker together make up Unit 1 (Figure 3-1).

The left inside front four man and the left inside linebacker together make up Unit 2 (Figure 3-2).

The right inside front four man and the right inside linebacker together make up Unit 3 (Figure 3-3).

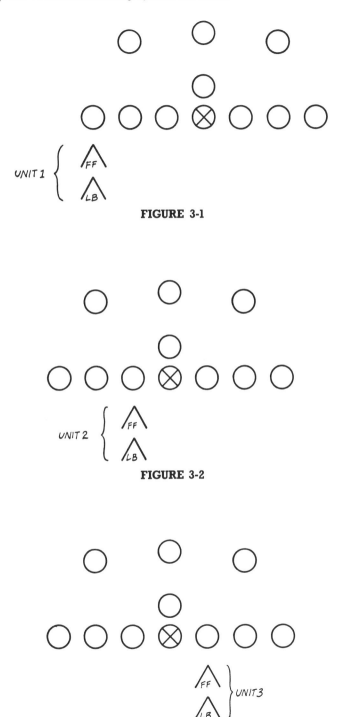

FIGURE 3-1

FIGURE 3-2

FIGURE 3-3

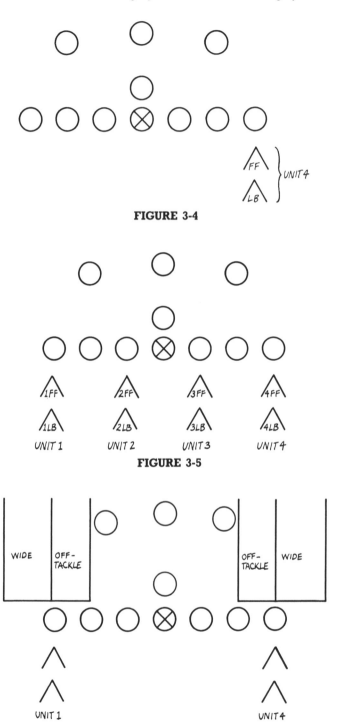

FIGURE 3-4

FIGURE 3-5

FIGURE 3-6

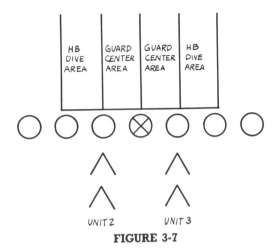

UNIT 2   UNIT 3

FIGURE 3-7

The right outside front four man and the right outside linebacker together make up Unit 4 (Figure 3-4).

Therefore, we have four units consisting of a front four man and a linebacker in each unit. As shown in Figure 3-5 we can now identify each of these defensive players as the number 2 linebacker (2LB) or number 4 front four man (4FF) or number 1 linebacker (1LB) or number 3 front four man (3FF).

Each unit is responsible for covering two offensive areas. Units 1 and 4 are responsible for the off-tackle areas and the immediate wide areas (Figure 3-6).

Units 2 and 3 are responsible for the halfback dive areas and the guard-center areas (Figure 3-7).

Each unit can work separately or with another unit to protect these areas.

BASIC UNIT PLAY

Before teaching any of the thirteen stunts of the 44 Stack defense, each of the four units should master the *basic play* of the unit. *The basic play of the unit is what each unit will do if not called on to execute a stunt.* Therefore, if only Units 1 and 3 are involved in a stunt, then Units 2 and 4 will *automatically* execute the basic play of the unit.

The front four man in the unit will use a forearm lift or a hand shiver when carrying out the basic unit play. His purpose is to neutralize the offensive end or guard in front of him and keep the end or guard off our linebackers and other defensive players. We like to use the forearm lift on medium- and short-yardage situations. In teaching the forearm lift we stress the following points:

1. Assume normal stance head-on the offensive end or guard.

2. Step towards the offensive player with the right foot (if the right forearm is to be used) or the left foot (if the left forearm is to be used).

3. Bring the forearm up into the numbers on the jersey of the offensive player.

4. Stop the charge of the offensive player and keep him away from defensive player's body.

5. Attempt to straighten the offensive player up and make him extend his legs. This takes away the leg drive and blocking force of the offensive player.

We want the front four man to use the hand shiver on long-yardage situations. This enables him to have more lateral pursuit. We stress the following points when teaching the hand shiver:

1. Step towards the offensive player and drive the heels of the hands into the offensive man's chest area just above and slightly outside the numbers.

2. Extend the arms and try to "raise the blocker up."

3. The front four man should keep his feet moving and keep the offensive player away from his body.

4. The elbows should be locked keeping the arms straight, and the fingers should be spread to provide a wide base and to enable the defensive player to maintain contact with the blocker.

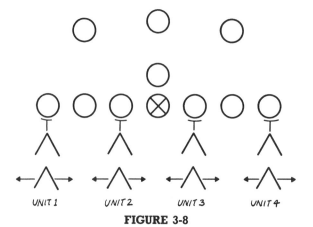

FIGURE 3-8

The basic play of the linebacker, when not called on to stunt, is relatively simple. The linebacker should stay in the stack position behind his front four man. He then reads the movement of the ball, being ready to move laterally right or left to protect his areas and make the tackle.

Figure 3-8 shows all four units in the *basic play* situation with the front four men using either the forearm lift or the hand shiver and the linebackers stacked behind them reacting to the ball and ready to protect their respective areas.

THE THIRTEEN BASIC STUNTS

"X" Stunt

The "X" is perhaps the most effective of our penetrating stunts. It involves both the front four man and the linebacker in the same unit. One of the two men will penetrate across the line of scrimmage through the gap to his right and the other will penetrate through the gap to his left. Both should step with the lead foot and penetrate low, hard, and fast into the offensive backfield, making absolutely certain they do not penetrate deeper than the ball.

The front four man and the linebacker have a number of ways they can execute the "X" stunt. Figure 3-9 shows Unit 1 X-ing. The front four man is taking the gap to his right and the linebacker is taking the gap to his left. The same unit is X-ing again in Figure 3-10, but the front four man and the linebacker have swapped gaps, with the front four man now going to his left and the linebacker going to his right.

It should be stated here that the linebacker always has the responsibility of telling the front four man which way to go. We instruct our

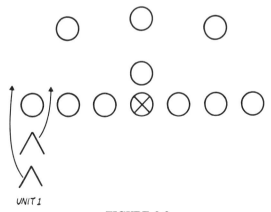

UNIT 1

FIGURE 3-9

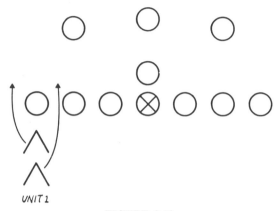

FIGURE 3-10

linebackers to give a *verbal* command of "go right" or "go left" to the front four man. This type of verbal command should be consistent with every unit so that whenever a substitute front four man is working with a linebacker there will be no possibility of confusion about *who* is to go which way. By all means, *never* allow the linebacker to pat the front four man on the back to indicate which way the front four man should go. The front four man could easily fail to understand the signal, and also there would be the danger of the offense seeing the hand signal and knowing that the stunt is coming.

The "X" stunt can be run from the stack position as in Figures 3-9 and 3-10 or from many different unit positions. Figure 3-11 shows Unit 1 X-ing from an off-set position. We have found this to be one of our best ways to run the "X" stunt. The off-set position makes it extremely difficult for the offensive tackle on the stunt side to block the linebacker because he has no assurance before the play starts that the linebacker is coming his way.

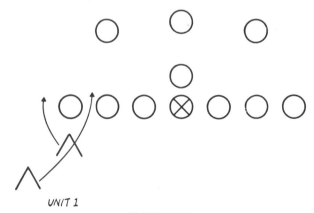

FIGURE 3-11

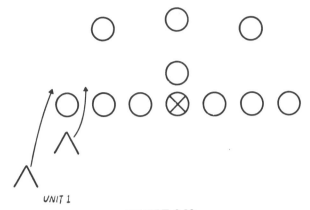

UNIT 1

FIGURE 3-12

Figure 3-12 shows the same off-set position and the same Unit 1 "X," but this time the linebacker penetrates outside the offensive end and the front four man goes inside.

Figure 3-13 shows a Unit 2 "X." The linebacker has told the front four man to cover the gap to his left. To make the defense look different the front four man has already lined up in the gap to his left with the linebacker stacked behind him. On the snap of the ball the front four man has only to go straight ahead and the linebacker stunt into his right gap. The same two players could line up in any reasonable position just as long as they cover their assigned gaps.

Two or more units may "X" at the same time. They can start from their natural stack position or can off-set or take any other position just so their positions allow them to penetrate their gaps. Figure 3-14 shows Units 2 and 3 X-ing, both from the normal stack position. Figure 3-15

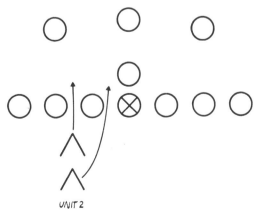

UNIT 2

FIGURE 3-13

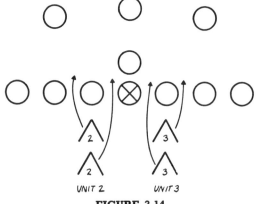

UNIT 2   UNIT 3

FIGURE 3-14

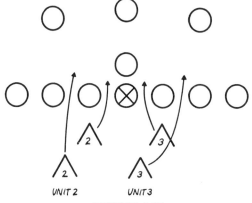

UNIT 2   UNIT 3

FIGURE 3-15

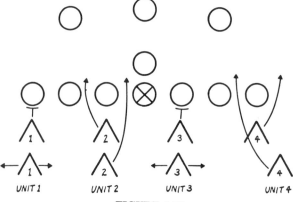

UNIT 1   UNIT 2   UNIT 3   UNIT 4

FIGURE 3-16

shows Units 2 and 3 X-ing again, but from different positions with different players penetrating different gaps.

Figure 3-16 shows all four units on defense. Units 2 and 4 are X-ing and Units 1 and 3 are in the basic play position (front four man is using forearm lift or hand shiver and linebacker is reading the play).

Figure 3-17 shows all units X-ing. As you can see, this becomes a *Gap-8* defense although it is perfectly hidden until the snap of the ball. The offense must be prepared to stop this stunt by having eight blockers available. If they don't, we will get someone into their backfield untouched.

As you have just seen, any number of units can be called on to "X" at any time. If we "X" one unit, we are *attacking* the offense with five men (four front men and one linebacker). If we "X" two units we are attacking the offense with six men (four front four men and two linebackers). Three units X-ing gives us a seven-man rush and, of course, all units X-ing gives us eight men attacking the offense. We have played and won games using only the "X" stunt during the entire game.

There are two important coaching points to consider when teaching the "X" stunt. First, make sure that the linebackers do not give away their intention to stunt by moving too quickly towards their gap *before* the ball is snapped. If they do this, the offensive linemen can see them and prepare to block them. Especially in the off-set position, the offensive lineman should have committed himself to a block a split second before the linebacker blasts through the gap. Secondly, make sure the units do not get patterns set up between the front four man and his linebacker where, for instance, the front four man takes the *inside* gap 95 percent of the time. They must even out the number of times each goes inside and outside so that the offensive line will always be guessing which one to try to block.

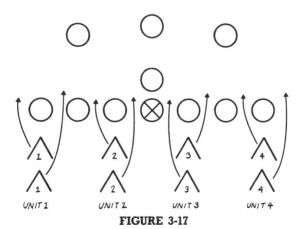

FIGURE 3-17

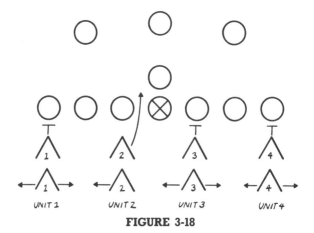

FIGURE 3-18

Gap Stunt

The *Gap* is a stunt performed only by a front four player. The Gap stunt is called when we want the front four man in a unit to penetrate a gap, but we want the linebacker to stay back, cover for him, and read the play. Figure 3-18 shows a Unit 2 Gap In call (*In* means in toward the center). The Unit 2 front four man has penetrated the gap to his inside. Now here is a very important coaching point—when the front four man is executing the Gap movement, the linebacker behind him should move laterally to cover the other gap that his unit is responsible for. In Figure 3-18 notice that the Unit 2 linebacker has moved to his left to protect his unit's other gap responsibility, although the linebacker does not penetrate. Also notice in Figure 3-18 that since they are not called on to stunt, Units 1, 3, and 4 are Basic.

The front four man should execute the Gap stunt exactly like he does the "X" stunt. He should step with the lead foot and penetrate into

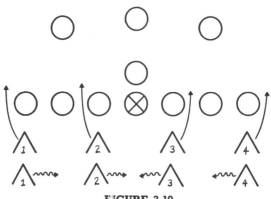

FIGURE 3-19

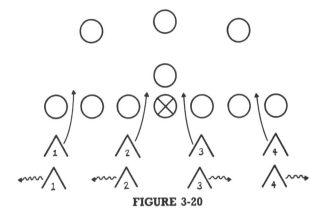

FIGURE 3-20

the offensive backfield as low, hard, and quickly as possible, making sure not to penetrate deeper than the ball.

Any combination of Gap stunts can be used. Figure 3-19 shows an All Gap Out stunt (*All* refers to all units, and *Out* means away from the center).

Figure 3-20 shows All Gap In.

Figure 3-21 is an illustration of Units 1 and 4 Gap In. Notice that Units 2 and 3 are Basic.

If you wanted the front four men to gap to the *wide side of the field,* the call could be All Gap Right (or Left). Figure 3-22 shows the wide side of the field to the right and an All Gap Right call.

If our opponent often uses a power set (all backs placed on one side of the offense), we could call All Gap to Power. We then take a look at their offense as they set up to see which way their power is. All front four men will then Gap in the direction of the power set. In Figure 3-23 the power is to our right and we are gapping our front four men in that direction, with the linebackers covering to their left.

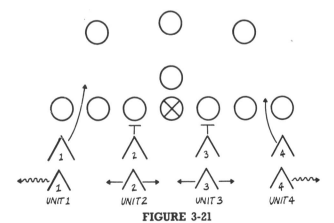

FIGURE 3-21

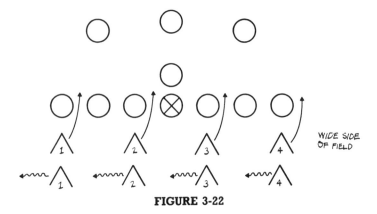

FIGURE 3-22

A strong point to remember is that when we call a stunt such as All Gap to Power, we must have good communication between all members of the defense so that we are all in agreement as to where the offensive power is.

Slant Stunt

This is an excellent way to keep the offensive tackles or center off our linebackers. The Slant is a stunt from head-on one offensive player to head-on another offensive player in an aggressive and surprising manner, and is performed by the front four men.

When teaching the Slant stunt as used in the 44 Stack defense, we first teach the front four man to line up slightly deeper off the line of scrimmage than usual. He should then step towards the offensive tackle or center with his lead foot, driving through the helmet of his opponent with his lead arm. The front four man should keep his feet wide apart and

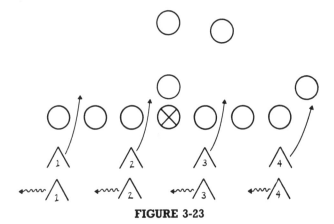

FIGURE 3-23

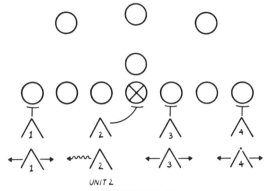

UNIT 2

FIGURE 3-24

moving as he drives for the far foot of his opponent. When Slanting, we do not want penetration as much as we want to neutralize the opponent.

Figure 3-24 shows Unit 2 Slant In. This call can be made if the center is effectively blocking our linebackers. Notice that as the Unit 2 front four man is Slanting, the Unit 2 linebacker has loosened up slightly and has moved laterally to his left. This is because he now has slightly more territory in his area to cover. All units, other than Unit 2, are Basic.

We could neutralize the offensive left tackle in either of two ways. We could call Unit 3 Slant Out (Figure 3-25). Or we could call Unit 4 Slant In (Figure 3-26).

On all Slant moves the linebacker behind the Slanting front four man must thoroughly understand that he is to move laterally in the opposite direction of the Slant and be prepared to cover slightly more area than normal.

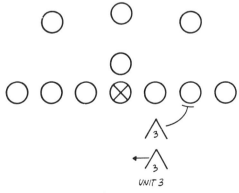

UNIT 3

FIGURE 3-25

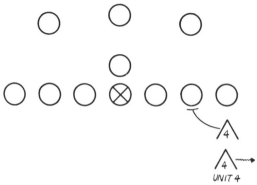

FIGURE 3-26

Loop Stunt

This stunt is very effective in stopping the off-tackle play and some wide plays. It involves the use of Units 1 and 2 working together *or* Units 3 and 4 working together. In the huddle we simply call Loop Left or Loop Right.

If we are running Loop Left, the Unit 1 front four man, on the snap, will slant into the offensive tackle. Sometimes we allow the Unit 1 front four man to cheat over a little to insure his getting to the offensive tackle as quickly as possible. The Unit 2 front four man will remain Basic and will deliver a forearm lift or hand shiver to the offensive guard. These two moves by the Unit 1 and Unit 2 front four players should neutralize the guard and tackle on the Loop side. The Unit 2 linebacker now fires off the tail of the Unit 1 front four man and heads straight for the offensive off-tackle hole. If the play is coming his way, the Unit 2 linebacker goes on through the hole into the offensive backfield. If the play is going away from him, the Unit 2 linebacker will stop and take the proper pursuit angle. The Unit 1 linebacker, on the snap of the ball, will move quickly to

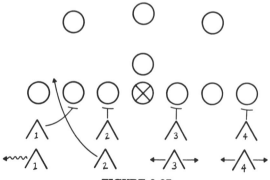

FIGURE 3-27

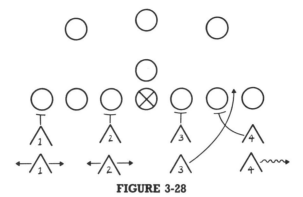

FIGURE 3-28

cover the wide area to his left. Figure 3-27 shows Loop Left. Notice that the players in Units 3 and 4 are Basic.

Figure 3-28 shows Loop Right and this time Units 1 and 2 are Basic. We have consistently found that the offense has a difficult time picking up the looping linebacker in time to block him effectively.

Fire Stunt

There are times when we want to fire a linebacker across the line of scrimmage, but keep the front four man playing Basic. We do this by calling a Fire stunt. In the huddle we might call Unit 3 Fire Out. This means the Unit 3 linebacker should penetrate hard and fast across the line of scrimmage going through the gap to his outside. On this stunt we want the front four man in the Firing unit to use the hand shiver, read the play, and be ready to move laterally. The front four man now has slightly more territory to cover since his linebacker has committed across the line of scrimmage. Figure 3-29 shows Unit 3 Fire Out. Notice that all units other than 3 are Basic.

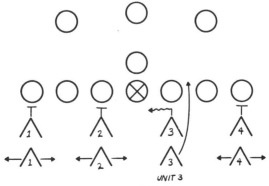

FIGURE 3-29

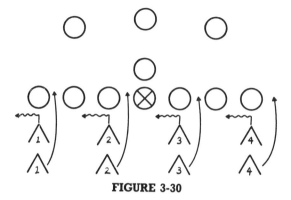

FIGURE 3-30

Figure 3-30 shows All Fire Right and would be a good call to the wide side of the field.

Against a team that uses a good many power set offensive plays, we could call All Fire to Power (Figure 3-31). This stunt would send all four linebackers stunting across the line in the direction of the offensive backs, and would have all four front four men using the hand shiver being ready to move laterally.

Figure 3-32 shows All Fire In.

Figure 3-33 shows All Fire Out.

Figure 3-34 shows Units 1 and 4 Fire In, Units 2 and 3 Fire Out.

The term Fire can also be used to stunt any of the three safety men across the line of scrimmage in a surprise move. Figure 3-35 shows Left Safety Fire Outside. To execute this stunt the left safety moves slowly toward the line of scrimmage as the quarterback prepares to call for the snap of the ball. On the snap the left safety fires across the line getting penetration as deep as the ball, and is careful not to let the ballcarrier get around him to the outside for a long gain. An extremely important

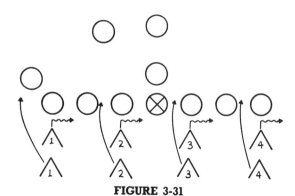

FIGURE 3-31

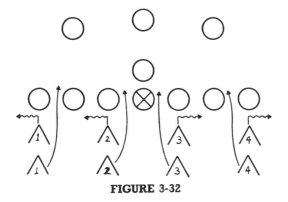

FIGURE 3-32

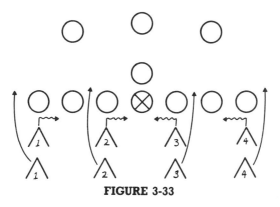

FIGURE 3-33

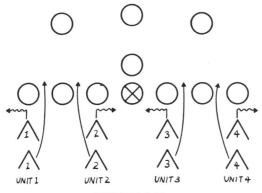

FIGURE 3-34

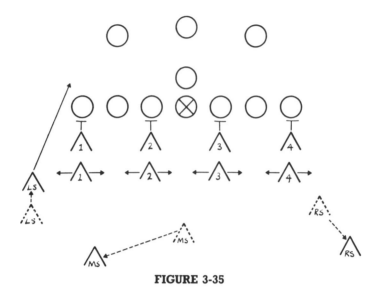

FIGURE 3-35

coaching point to stress is this: when *any* safety is in a Firing stunt, the other two safeties must shift quickly to a two-deep zone coverage about 12 yards deep and contain against a possible long run or pass.

Figure 3-36 shows Right Safety Fire Off-Tackle. The right safety should casually move up to within about five or six yards of the line of scrimmage and position himself just outside the Unit 4 linebacker. On the snap he fires hard into the offensive off-tackle area looking for the ball. The offense will find it hard to block this safety because the defense has neutralized their guard and end with the Basic play of Units 3 and 4 and their tackle should have no idea the Safety Fire is coming. The left safety and middle safety must thoroughly understand what the right safety is doing so that they can adjust to their two-deep zone.

Middle Safety Fire Right Middle is a good up-the-middle stunt by a safety and is shown in Figure 3-37. To best open an alley for the middle safety, Unit 2 should execute an "X" stunt and the front four man in Unit 3 should Gap Out. The middle safety must be careful not to prematurely give away his intention to stunt so that no blocker will plan to block him. When the middle safety is firing, the left and right safety men cover two-deep zone.

In Figure 3-38, the middle safety is Firing the Left Middle. Unit 3 will now "X" and Unit 2 will Gap Out to open the alley for the middle safety.

Fire and Delay Stunt

Sometimes in order to confuse blocking assignments to the outside, we will fire both the left safety and the right safety and drop the Unit 1

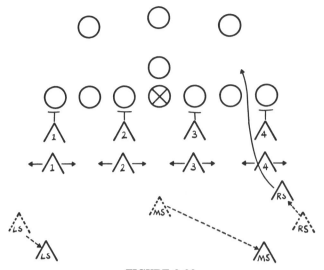

FIGURE 3-36

and Unit 4 linebackers off the line of scrimmage to play ⅓ deep pass defense. The dropping off of the linebackers is the "delay" part of the stunt. In carrying out this stunt the outside safety men should get slightly closer to the line of scrimmage than usual and the linebackers on the outside must be ready to quickly take ⅓ field responsibility. Figure 3-39 shows Fire and Delay Left and Fire and Delay Right. We have the Unit 1 and Unit 4 front four players gapping to their inside to protect the off-tackle area. Naturally, this stunt should rarely be used when the offense has a wide flanker or split end to one side because of the danger of a quick pass to him before the outside linebacker can provide coverage.

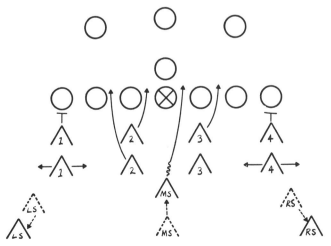

FIGURE 3-37

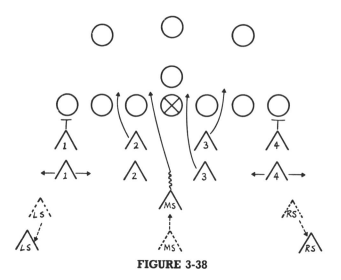

FIGURE 3-38

Pass Rush to the Split End Stunt

This is a stunt we use against a team that uses a split end often. The purpose of this stunt is to put quick pressure on the passer and force him to throw quickly or risk not getting his pass off. After calling this stunt, the defensive players must recognize the split end side as the offense

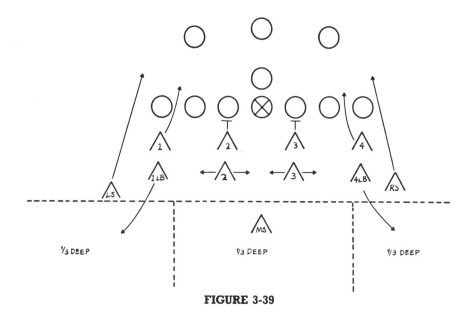

FIGURE 3-39

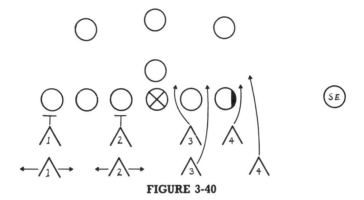

FIGURE 3-40

breaks the huddle. Our defensive players should call "right" or "left" so that all are aware of the split end side.

Figure 3-40 shows the split end to our right. The Unit 4 front four man has moved in to the outside shoulder of the offensive tackle. The Unit 4 linebacker stays in his normal position. On the snap, Unit 3 will penetrate their gaps as shown (this is actually an "X"). The Unit 4 front four man and linebacker will rush the passer as shown, making sure they keep the passer inside of them. The players in Units 1 and 2 are Basic. This stunt should give us more defensive players than blockers on this side. Figure 3-41 shows the same stunt with the split end on our left.

Linebackers Wide Stunt

This is a simple movement that gives the defense a different look. It is a good long-yardage play. It tends to keep the entire offense inside the total defensive area and it discourages the offense from trying to run

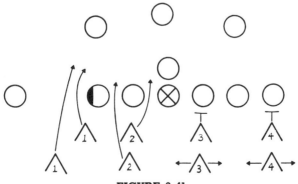

FIGURE 3-41

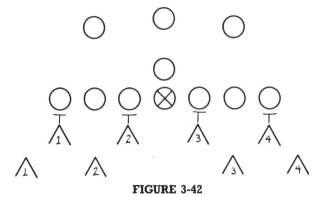

FIGURE 3-42

wide. When Linebackers Wide is called (Figure 3-42), all linebackers should stay in the stack position until just before the snap. At this time all linebackers will quickly move 1 to 1½ yards to their outside and await the snap of the ball. It is not a penetrating stunt. All front four men will play Basic. If desired, any number of units can be moved wide. Figure 3-43 shows Units 1 and 4 Linebackers Wide. Notice that Units 2 and 3 will remain in the Basic play stack position.

Crash Stunt

This stunt helps stop the off-tackle play, yet still gives us good coverage to the outside. It is executed by the players in Unit 1 or the players in Unit 4. As the quarterback approaches the center and prepares to take the snap, the Unit 1 or Unit 4 linebacker (depending on which side the stunt is called to) moves out and up towards the line of scrimmage. When the ball is snapped the linebacker penetrates quickly across the line of scrimmage, coming down the line of scrimmage on the offensive

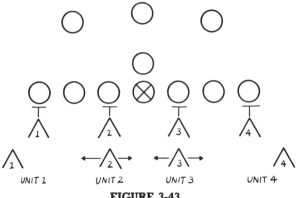

FIGURE 3-43

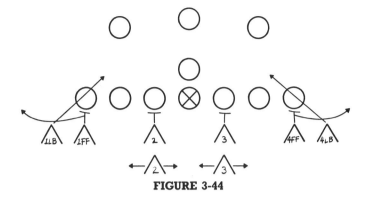

FIGURE 3-44

side of the off-tackle area. The linebacker must come straight down the line hard and fast or the play could be by him before he gets there. He also leaves himself open for an easy block if he doesn't come down the line hard and tough. The front four player on the Crash side uses a quick hand shiver and slides to the outside to cover the immediate wide area. Figure 3-44 shows Crash Left and Crash Right.

Stack Right, Left, In, or Out Stunt

This defensive call provides for the movement of a unit into an offensive gap just before the snap. This movement will provide strength for our defense at that gap and also will confuse blocking assignments. A single unit or any number of units can be called on to position themselves into gaps. When a unit is stacked in a gap, the front four man will penetrate straight through the gap and the linebacker will find the ball and pursue.

Figure 3-45 shows All Stack Right. Although this might look weak to our left side it could be that we are trying to cover the wide side of the

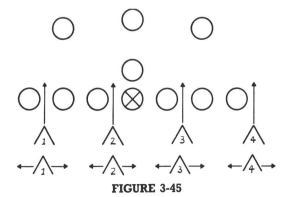

FIGURE 3-45

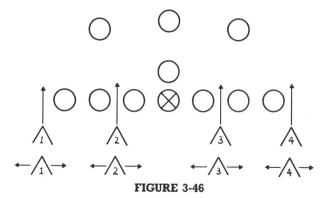

FIGURE 3-46

field to our right. Or maybe we are trying to force the offense to run back to our left side where we are physically stronger than our opponents.

Figure 3-46 shows All Stack Out. We can call this on long-yardage situations when we believe the offense will not try to run up the middle. Figure 3-47 shows Units 3 and 4 Stack Out. This does not affect Units 1 and 2 and they will play Basic or engage in another stunt.

Delay Ends Stunt

This stunt is to be used against a team that passes frequently to its tight ends. It is a stunt used by Units 1 and 4 only. The front four man should line up head-on or slightly outside the tight end. On the snap the front four man will forearm lift or hand shiver (whichever he can do more effectively) the tight end and knock him inside towards the offensive tackle. The front four man should attempt to maintain contact with the tight end for about two seconds before releasing him. After releasing him the front four player proceeds to rush the passer. We feel these two seconds are sufficient to destroy the timing between passer and receiver.

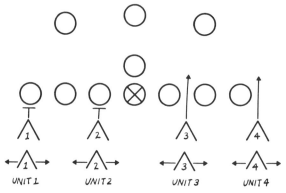

FIGURE 3-47

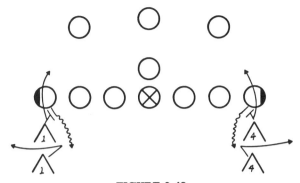

FIGURE 3-48

The linebacker on the Delay End side checks to see that the tight end has been hit by the front four man. If for some reason the front four man was unable to do his job, the linebacker should attempt to make brief legal contact with the tight end before taking his pass defense position.

Delay Ends—Both Sides is illustrated in Figure 3-48. The front four player must try to make the tight end release inside so that he can get a good shot at knocking him inside. If the tight end is able to release to the *outside* of the front four man, the linebacker should be in position to make legal contact with the tight end briefly before taking his pass defense position.

Figure 3-49 shows the tight end releasing outside the front four player. Make sure that the front four man understands that if the tight end does release outside of him he should *not* chase the tight end just trying to get a shot at delaying him. The front four man should go ahead with this pass rush leaving the delay of the tight end to the linebacker.

All Units Loose Position

We use this quite often on long-yardage situations, especially in situations such as 3rd and over 8 yards to go for a first down. We feel that

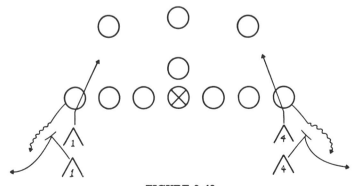

FIGURE 3-49

we can play loose and give up 5 or 6 yards if necessary just so the offense does not break the long run or pass on us. We are willing to stay back a little, read the offensive play, and pursue the ballcarrier, holding him short of the first down. This usually results in the offense having to punt.

At first glance, the All Units Loose position will resemble the previously described Linebackers Wide position. However, there are several major differences. First, the front four men use the hand shiver at all times when playing All Units Loose. This is because the hand shiver offers better pursuit by the front four men. Second, the linebackers get a little wider and 4 or 5 yards off the line of scrimmage so that the ballcarrier cannot get by them quickly. Third, the three safety men line up 2 to 4 yards deeper than usual. It is recommended that this loosening up of the linebackers and safety men not be shown until the quarterback has taken his position under the center and is about to take the snap. Figure 3-50 shows the All Units Loose Position.

Jam Stunt

This is one defensive move which we do not have to use often, but we like to have it when we need it. We are all aware that a good defensive player gets double-teamed often. The Jam is a double-team by the defense on an offensive player, especially one who is having success against us. For example, let's say the offensive tackle on our left side is having a good game blocking us. He could be a big strong player who is really clearing a path for the ballcarrier and the offense is running behind him often. We could call Jam Tackle—Left Side. On the snap of the ball our Unit 1 and Unit 2 front four men would both execute a slant movement into the tackle. This almost assures us of neutralizing any block he is attempting to make and also quite often leads us to the play. It is very important that the linebackers behind these front four players be taught to play a little

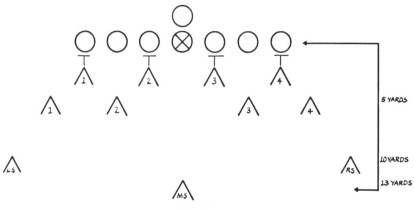

FIGURE 3-50

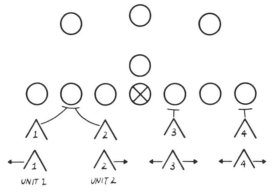

FIGURE 3-51

more loosely than usual for they now have a larger area to protect. We have found it best not to call the Jam stunt when a short-yardage situation is in order because the front four men should be putting all their effort into Jamming the tackle rather than watching for a quick hitting play. We feel that the Jam stunt gives the offensive lineman something to worry about in that he never knows when this stunt might be used against him.

Figure 3-51 illustrates the Jam Tackle—Left Side stunt. (The front four men in Unit 3 and Unit 4 would work together to Jam the Tackle on the Right Side.)

To Jam the Center we must use the front four men of Unit 2 and Unit 3 (Figure 3-52).

When we wish to Jam an offensive end or guard we must use a front four man and his linebacker. To Jam an end the front four man moves to the inside shoulder of the offensive end and the linebacker moves to the end's outside shoulder. They both deliver a forearm lift to the end to neutralize his block. Figure 3-53 illustrates Jam Ends—Both Sides.

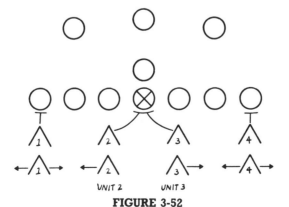

FIGURE 3-52

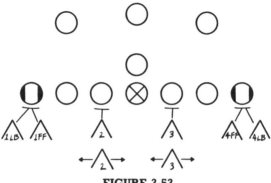

FIGURE 3-53

To Jam an offensive guard, the front four man who usually lines up head-on the guard will move to the inside shoulder of the guard. The linebacker in the same unit moves up to the guard's outside shoulder. They both deliver a forearm lift to the offensive guard to neutralize his block. Figure 3-54 shows Jam Guards—Both Sides.

Remember: The offensive tackles and center are Jammed by front four men only. The offensive ends and guards are Jammed by a front four player and his linebacker.

COMBINING STUNTS

Any two or more of the previously described stunts can be combined on a single defensive play. For example, we can run an "X" stunt with Unit 2 and a Crash stunt with Unit 4. This gives the 44 Stack defense a great deal of flexibility. There are actually hundreds of stunt combinations that can be derived by matching up two or more of the stunts described in this chapter.

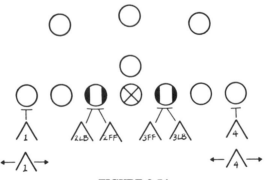

FIGURE 3-54

In preparing a defensive game plan, select those stunts and stunt combinations that will place players in position to stop the favorite plays of the opponent. Then, as the game gets underway, you can use these stunt combinations or easily piece together *new* stunt combinations to best stop the opponent's offense. There are very few defenses which can claim this much flexibility. It is also important to note that the players will not need to have practiced every stunt *combination* that might be needed in a game. Just so they can execute the thirteen stunts they will have no problem. For example, in a game the defense might need to run Loop Left, 3 Gap Out, Crash Right in order to best close the opponent's running lanes. This will present no problem as each unit will execute its stunt separate from what the others are doing.

A good coaching point to remember is that it is often best to combine stunts leaving at least one linebacker *not* stunting, especially on long-yardage situations. This linebacker can play a little more loosely than normal and watch for plays such as the draw or the screen pass.

Figures 3-55 through Figure 3-60 show examples of how stunts can be combined.

Figure 3-55 ... 2 "X," Loop Right

Figure 3-56 ... 1 and 4 Crash, 2 and 3 "X."

Figure 3-57 ... 2 or 3 "X," Pass Rush to the Split End.

(Note: We must say "2 *or* 3 X" because we will not know which side the Pass Rush will be to until the offense breaks the huddle. If the Pass Rush is to the right, then Unit 2 will "X." If the Pass Rush is to the left, then Unit 3 will "X".)

Figure 3-58 ... Linebackers Wide, 1 Gap In, 3 "X."

Figure 3-59 ... Fire and Delay Both Sides, 2 and 3 "X."

Figure 3-60 ... Pass Rush to Split End Side, Crash to Tight End Side.

We have found that all these stunt variations create a great deal of doubt in an offensive player's mind about which player to block. And the more doubt we create in his mind about which player to block, the less chance he will have to make a successful block!

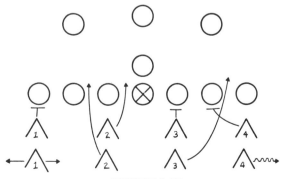

FIGURE 3-55

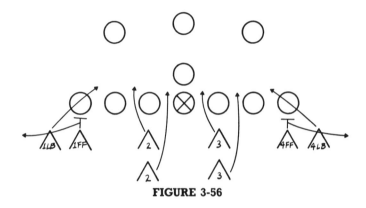

FIGURE 3-56

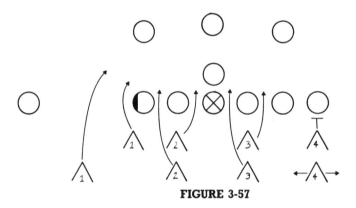

FIGURE 3-57

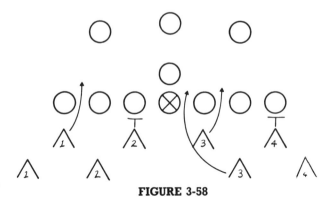

FIGURE 3-58

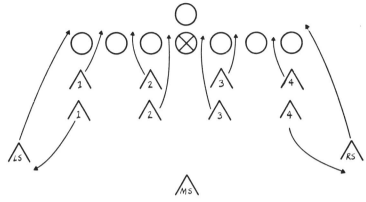

FIGURE 3-59

WHEN SHOULD STUNTS BE CALLED?

The 44 Stack *is designed* to be a stunting defense. The more the players stunt, the better the defense is, just as long as the stunts are called intelligently. That is, thought should be given to why each stunt is called and what is to be accomplished by calling a particular stunt. Stunts should be called *anywhere* on the field from the opponent's 1-yard line to deep in the defensive team's territory. They should be called on 1st, 2nd, 3rd, and 4th down. Stunts can be used very effectively to rush a punt.

In our first year with the 44 Stack, we tried to play one opponent by giving our 44 Stack players a considerable number of "keys" to watch for and react to, and we cut down on the number of stunts we used. However, we found that these "keys" tended to keep our players stationary too long and kept us from playing aggressive, stunting football. Consequently, we lost the game and learned a lesson. We aren't saying "keys" aren't important. They are. But select only those "keys" that are absolutely

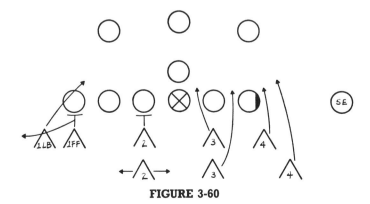

FIGURE 3-60

necessary, make intelligent stunt selections, then turn the players loose to play stunting, aggressive football.

Calling Off Stunts

There are times when a particular stunt that has been called in the defensive huddle should be called off at the line of scrimmage. The defensive players should be prepared for this and be ready to make the proper adjustment.

When the offensive team approaches the line of scrimmage and the defensive team sees that the planned stunt would not be beneficial, all defensive players should call *"Normal."* On hearing this, all defensive players should play a Basic 44 Stack with no stunt. For example, if Pass Rush to the Split End has been called in the huddle, but the offense lines up with two tight ends, "Normal" should be called. As the defensive team gets more experience in playing the 44 Stack, the players will be able to *substitute* stunts at the line of scrimmage.

Calling Stunts at the Line of Scrimmage

We do not recommend that the defensive players call stunts at the line of scrimmage (after the offense has committed itself to a certain formation) until the players are thoroughly familiar with all facets of the 44 Stack defense. By the end of the first year of use, or at least by the second year, the defensive players should be able to call at least some stunts after the offense has set up. It is an advantage, of course, if the defensive players can do this. Let's say that the opponent (according to the scouting report) has had success with a sweep play or a peel play (both

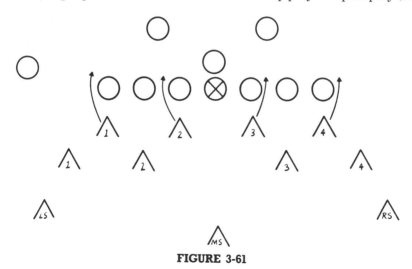

FIGURE 3-61

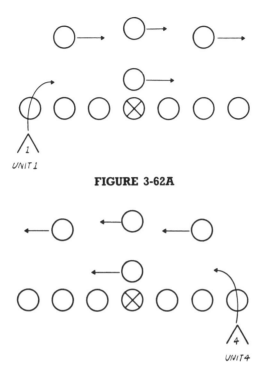

FIGURE 3-62A

FIGURE 3-62B

wide plays) whenever they have a flanker to our left and a split backfield. Therefore, when this formation is seen by the defensive players, the defensive signal caller can call a stunt that places players in position to stop the sweep or peel play. As shown in Figure 3-61, a good call would be Linebackers Wide, All Gap Out. The offense may not run the sweep or the peel play, but at least the defense has the percentage in its favor and has not had to call the defense until the offense showed its formation. Being able to call defensive signals at the line of scrimmage will also depend a great deal on the intelligence and alertness of the defensive signal caller.

PURSUIT ANGLES WHEN NOT STUNTING

Any player on the 44 Stack defense who is *not* stunting has a definite pursuit angle which he should know thoroughly so that the defense can be kept sound. Figures 3-62A and 3-62B show the pursuit angles on the Unit 1 and Unit 4 front four men. Their pursuit angle is *behind* the line of scrimmage on the offensive side.

Figures 3-63A and 3-63B show the pursuit angles of the Unit 2 and Unit 3 front four players. They hit and pursue on the defensive side of the line of scrimmage.

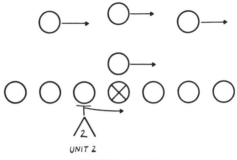

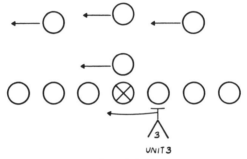

UNIT 2

FIGURE 3-63A

UNIT 3

FIGURE 3-63B

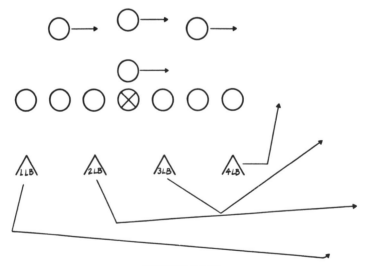

FIGURE 3-64A

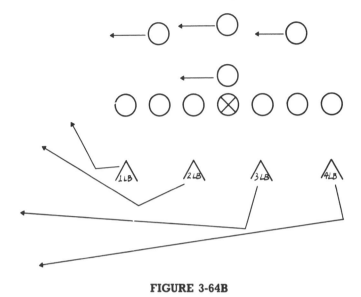

FIGURE 3-64B

Figures 3-64A and 3-64B show the pursuit angles of all four linebackers.

Figures 3-65A and 3-65B show the pursuit angles of the three safety men. Notice that each stays in his ⅓ deep pass defense area until all threat of a pass is gone before pursuing the ballcarrier.

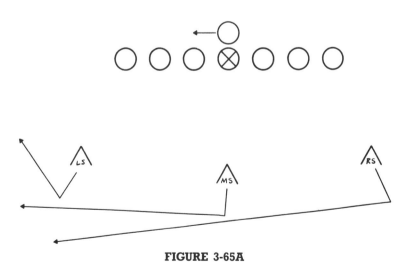

FIGURE 3-65A

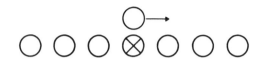

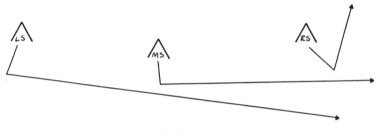

FIGURE 3-65B

4

Coaching the 44 Stack Pass Defense

The 44 Stack defense, if played properly, provides the most complete and flexible pass coverage of any defense. From three to seven pass defenders can be utilized on pass defense on any particular play. The number of players to be used on pass defense is not known to the offense until the ball is in play. This makes pass play-calling difficult since the quarterback doesn't know what type of pass defense he will face. We may rush the passer with eight defensive players and retain three pass defenders or we may rush the passer with only the front four and retain seven pass defenders. We can use zone pass coverage or play a tight man-to-man coverage. The 44 Stack defense is easily adjusted to cover flankers, split ends, or two wide receivers on the same side.

THE PLAY OF THE FRONT FOUR MEN ON PASS DEFENSE

Pass defense starts with a good pass rush. Often, a defensive team will work for hours each week preparing the defensive backs and linebackers for the passing attack of their opponent, but will leave the pass rush to chance. The rush of the defensive line can be the biggest factor in the success or failure of an opponent's passing attack. The front four linemen are the leaders in our 44 Stack pass rush. They are often aided by stunting linebackers. However, the main responsibility of rushing the passer belongs to the front four.

When planning a pass rush, the front four should be informed in detail about the type of passes they can expect from the offense. Some teams use only *drop-back* passes. Some prefer the *roll-out* or *sprint-out* passes while other teams use *play-action* passes entirely. A well-balanced offense will contain some of each type of pass play. The front four should be coached as to the types of passes the offense is expected to use if the pass rush is to be effective.

When anticipating a pass, or against a team that passes a great deal, we want each front four man to line up as close to the line of scrimmage as possible because the front four man is to attempt to get past the offensive blocker before the blocker has time to set up in his pass-blocking position. When teaching the pass rush, we ask each front four man to hand shiver the blocker under the shoulder pads and attempt to straighten him up. He should then accelerate through the blocker using power so that the blocker will be kept off-balance. The defender should use as much leg drive as possible to get past the blocker and should use his hands to ward off the blocking attempts of his opponent. It should be stressed with each front four man that the *hands* are a great defensive weapon. When used legally, the hands can be used to great advantage by the defensive player in getting past the blocker. If the blocker continues to make contact, the front four player should try to overpower him or roll around him, making sure to keep the passer to the inside.

We do not teach the front four defenders to begin their pass rush with their hands and arms raised. This tends to slow down the rush by the defender. It does not allow the defender to use his hands in warding off the blocker. It also gives the offensive lineman a larger blocking area to shoot for as he attempts to block, and often the block is made in the vulnerable rib cage area causing injury to the defender.

Once the defender has gotten past the blocker, he should keep in front of the passer so the passer has to throw *over* him. As the passer gets set to throw, the defender, now free of the blocker, should raise his hands and arms to hinder the view of the passer and possibly block the pass. The defender should rarely, if ever, leave his feet or jump up in an attempt to block the pass. This leaves the defender off balance and provides the passer with a fine opportunity to fake the pass and run.

As the front four players rush the passer, they should rush from the *outside*, always keeping the passer to their inside. This prevents the passer from escaping around the end for a possible long run. If the passer does decide to run, it is much better for him to run up the middle where defenders can close in from all sides. Figure 4-1 shows the proper pass rush angles of the front four.

The Unit 1 and Unit 4 front four men should notice that often the offensive end, lined up head-on them, will release for a pass when a pass play is called. This frees the Unit 1 and Unit 4 front four men to rush quickly across the line of scrimmage and into the backfield. Usually a

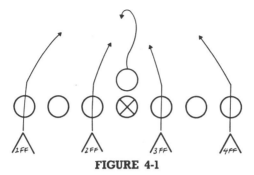

FIGURE 4-1

back will be waiting to block the front four man on his side in an effort to protect the passer. The front four man should use the same techniques in getting past this backfield blocker that he used to get past the offensive lineman. *Coaching point to remember:* It is seldom beneficial for the Unit 1 or Unit 4 front four player to attempt to dodge around the backfield blocker. This usually takes the defender out of range of making the tackle and can create an alley for the passer to run through.

Since the 44 Stack defense is designed as a stunting defense, more often than not we will supplement the pass rush of the front four with the stunting of from one to four linebackers. There are several excellent stunts described in Chapter 3 that can put quick pressure on the passer. A good scouting report will often indicate a weak pass blocker. The defense should prepare a game plan designed to stunt heavily through this area.

One of the most important tasks of a front four player is learning to recognize and play the screen pass. The Unit 1 and Unit 4 front four men are mainly responsible for "reading" a screen pass to the outside. The Units 2 and 3 front four men must learn to recognize the screen up the middle.

In playing a screen pass to the outside the Unit 1 or Unit 4 front four defender should begin to rush the passer as usual. As he rushes he should watch for two things: (1) a half-effort block by a lineman or back followed by quick movement away from the defender, and (2) the passer dropping back deeper than the normal seven or eight yards' passing depth. If either of these things (or in most cases both of these things) is happening, the front four player should consider the possibility of a screen and look quickly to the outside to see if a screen is being set up. Often a back will make the half-effort screen block on the Unit 1 or Unit 4 defender and the defender can "read" it and turn and go right with the back into the wall of the screen. Figure 4-2 shows the Unit 1 front four player reading a halfback screen to the outside. The front four player should turn and go with the halfback leaving the pass rush to the other front four defenders.

Figure 4-3 shows a fullback screen up the middle. The Units 2 and 3

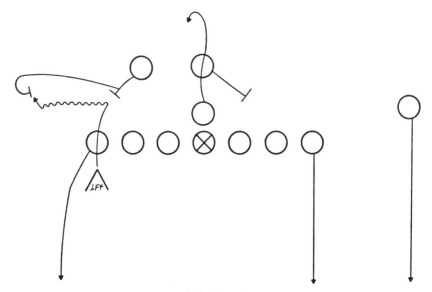

FIGURE 4-2

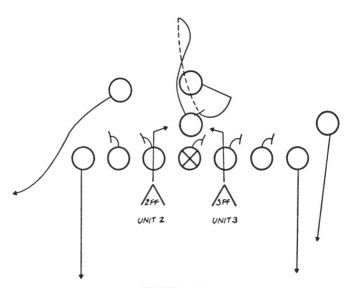

FIGURE 4-3

front four players should "feel" the screen block by the offensive linemen and attempt to remain in the center of the screen.

The linebackers will also be able to aid in recognizing and playing the screen, but the first move must belong to the front four men. Daily work on reading the screen will help eliminate this potentially dangerous play.

The front four should also be alert for the *draw* play to the fullback or to a halfback. There are several ways the draw play can be run and a good scouting report should indicate the way the opponent prefers to run it. In teaching our front four to control the draw play, we stress the importance of keeping the football in view at all times while rushing the quarterback. If this is done, the front four player seldom has trouble picking up the draw play. If the front four defender has any question as to whether the quarterback has handed the football to a running back on the draw play, he should tackle the running back. It is better to tackle the running back, even if he doesn't have the football, and rush the passer with fewer men, than to bypass a running back who possibly has been given the ball.

COMMUNICATION BETWEEN LINEBACKERS AND SAFETY MEN

No pass defense is sound unless those men playing pass defense are constantly in communication with each other. This communication should begin as the offensive team breaks their huddle. As soon as a defensive player recognizes the offensive formation, he should identify it to his teammates. His teammates should then join with him in naming the offensive formation to insure that all eleven defensive players clearly recognize and understand the formation. The defenders should call out such information as "split end left, I formation," or "slot right, split backfield," or "unbalanced line to our left with full-house backfield."

If the defense has been properly coached as to the offensive tendencies when aligned in certain formations, the defensive players should begin alerting teammates of certain possible plays to look for. For instance, perhaps the offensive team has shown a tendency to favor a halfback dive play, a sweep around end and a reverse when aligned in a slot left, split backfield formation (Figure 4-4). The defenders should call "slot left, split backfield . . . watch dive, sweep, or reverse."

If the offensive team has a certain back or end who is extremely dangerous, you may wish to instruct your defensive players to call the position of this player as well as to call any special instructions about this player. For instance, the defenders can help each other by saying, "*Johnson* at left halfback. Watch the halfback pass," or "*Williams* at

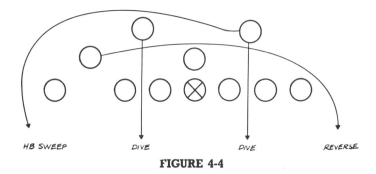

HB SWEEP   DIVE   DIVE   REVERSE

FIGURE 4-4

wingback. Watch out for the reverse back this way." Or the defenders may say, "Number 88 is in at right end. Watch him on the end around or the quick pass over the middle."

It is our belief that, as each defender hears his teammates calling out formations and players to watch for, he gains more confidence in himself. The defender feels that the defense has been properly prepared for anything the offense plans to try. It should also be a bit discouraging to the offense if every time they break the huddle they can hear the defenders calling out their formations and play tendencies.

A good coaching point is that you should instruct your defenders on exactly what to watch for and call out. If you don't, the players may do too much talking which leads to confusion and cuts down on the aggressiveness of the defenders. Intelligent communication is needed. Unnecessary talk should be eliminated.

Since linebackers and safety men are always in a stand-up position where they can see, and since they have the responsibility of covering flankers, split ends, etc., they are given a major share of the responsibility for communication in the 44 Stack defense. They must accept communication as part of their job if the defense is to be sound.

PLAYING THE 44 STACK ZONE PASS DEFENSE

Unless we specifically call for a man-to-man coverage in the huddle, or unless we are forced into an automatic man-to-man pass coverage by the offense at the line, we always play a zone pass defense. As stated in Chapter 1, one of the major goals of the 44 Stack is to *stop the long touchdown run or pass*. The best way to accomplish this is to utilize the zone type of pass coverage. As explained later in the chapter, we do use a man-to-man coverage at times, but we use it as a change-up type of pass coverage when we feel it is needed.

The basic idea of the zone type of pass coverage is to assign each linebacker and safety man a certain area or territory to cover should the offense call a passing play. When the passing play begins to develop, each pass defender moves into his territory and covers any receiver who enters his area. If two potential receivers come into the area assigned to one defender, the defender should cover the *deeper* receiver in his area.

Play of the Outside Linebackers in Zone Pass Defense

The two outside linebackers have the most difficult position to play in the zone pass defense in that they, quicker than any other defender, must identify the play as a run or a pass. Failure to do this properly could cause problems for the defense. A great deal of practice time is necessary if the outside linebacker is to learn to identify and play the run or pass properly. This is why two of the team's better athletes should be placed at the outside linebacker positions.

The quickest way for the outside linebacker to determine if the play is a pass or a run is to key the offensive end, wingback, or slotback on his side. If this player *releases* downfield, it usually means that he is going out for a pass or is going downfield to block (which probably indicates the play is a run to the other side). Therefore, the outside linebacker should move to his zone pass defense area checking for a pass or being ready to take his proper pursuit in case of a run. If the end, wingback, or slotback on his side blocks, this usually indicates a run to that side, and the outside linebacker can come up to protect against the run.

Once the outside linebacker has identified the play as a pass, he covers the flat area to a depth of 7 to 8 yards as shown in Figure 4-5. The outside linebacker should pick up any potential receiver coming into his area and stay with him until the receiver leaves his area or until the ball is thrown. Once the ball has been thrown, the defender reacts to the ball, leaving his zone if necessary.

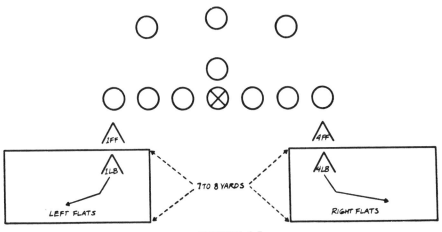

FIGURE 4-5

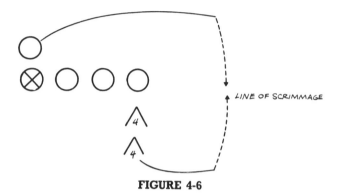

FIGURE 4-6

In playing the sprint-out or roll-out type of pass, the outside linebacker should first take his zone pass defense position. He should try to stay as deep off the line of scrimmage as the passer is deep on the other side of the line. Therefore, if the passer should decide to run instead of throw, the outside linebacker should be able to meet the passer as he gets to the line of scrimmage. The defender can now make the tackle on or near the line for little or no gain (Figure 4-6).

If the pass play develops *away* from an outside linebacker, that linebacker should continue to cover his zone watching for a throwback pass (Figure 4-7). When it is clear that no throwback pass is developing, the outside linebacker can leave his zone and take his proper pursuit angle.

The outside linebacker, when covering his pass area in the flat, is usually in good position to see a screen pass to the outside developing. When the passer releases the ball to the receiver behind the screen wall,

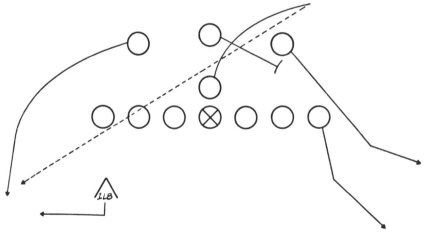

FIGURE 4-7

the outside linebacker comes up hard in an effort to break up the screen and make the tackle.

Since outside linebackers are often called on to stunt across the line of scrimmage, their flat pass defense areas will sometimes be left unguarded. Even if a pass is called in the flat area when the outside linebacker is stunting, the extra pressure put on the passer by the surprise rush of the linebacker will make it difficult for the passer to select a receiver in the vacated area and throw accurately to him. Even if the pass is complete, we prefer giving up the short pass to a longer one. The number of times the outside linebacker stunt catches the passer for a loss will more than make up for yardage gained by the offense by passing in the vacated flat area.

Play of the Inside Linebackers in Zone Pass Defense

When not stunting, the two inside linebackers are in good position to cover the short pass areas over the middle. The inside linebackers should look for the block of the guard or tackle nearest them to determine if the play is a pass or a run. If the play is a run, the guards and tackles will fire out hard and try to drive the defenders off the line of scrimmage. If a pass play is developing, the guards and tackles will show pass blocking, but will not be able to release downfield. The inside linebackers should spend considerable practice time learning to read the pass block techniques of guards and tackles.

Upon reading the pass block the inside linebackers should go immediately to their pass defense zones as shown in Figure 4-8. These zones should extend to a depth of 8 to 10 yards. As the linebackers drop back in their areas, they should angle to the outside. If both linebackers dropped straight back, the area of coverage would be smaller and tend to overlap (Figure 4-9).

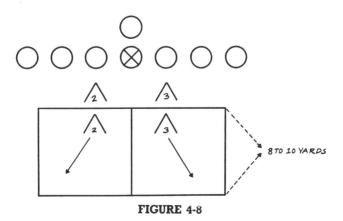

FIGURE 4-8

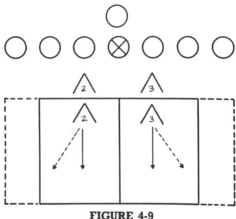

FIGURE 4-9

As the linebackers drop back, they should be looking for any potential receiver cutting through their area. These eligible receivers should be hit legally by the linebackers to disrupt their pass patterns; however, make sure the linebackers understand that the receiver cannot be hit if the pass has already been thrown and the ball is in flight. Figure 4-10 shows two potential receivers being hit by inside linebackers as they attempt to run their patterns in the short middle area.

If one linebacker is stunting, the other inside linebacker must be aware of the fact that he now must take a different position for pass defense. This remaining linebacker must position himself to cover the entire middle short zone as shown in Figure 4-11. Here is a good example of how communication between linebackers is important. The stunting linebacker should always remind the remaining linebacker that he has the entire middle short area to himself should a pass play develop.

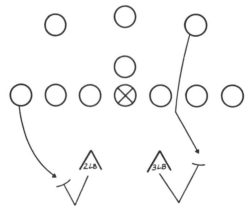

FIGURE 4-10

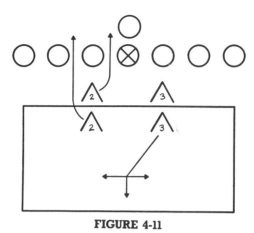

FIGURE 4-11

What happens if both inside linebackers are stunting and a pass play develops in the short middle zone where the inside linebackers normally cover? There certainly is the possibility that the pass might be complete. In fact, this was one of the biggest questions we had when we first began to design our 44 Stack defense. However, we found time and again in practice situations and in actual game situations that the stunting of our inside linebackers caused more damage to the offense than the few times when the pass over the middle was called and completed. We still have the three safety men to prevent the play from going for the touchdown even if the pass is complete. *Remember:* the quarterback must call the "pass over the middle" on the exact play that we have both inside linebackers stunting, and he must overcome the surprise rush of both inside linebackers and complete the pass before we can feel we have been hurt by leaving the short middle zone vacated.

The inside linebackers are given the responsibility of watching for the *draw* play which often develops in a passing situation. If the quarterback starts to drop back as if to pass, both inside linebackers should take their zones keeping the ball in view. If a draw play develops, both linebackers should be in good position to come up and help make the tackle. If the Unit 2 linebacker is stunting, we give the Unit 3 linebacker the responsibility of checking for the draw play should it occur, and vice versa.

The inside linebackers must also be alert for the screen pass up the middle. When the offensive linemen let our front four through easily and begin to form the screen wall in the middle, the inside linebackers should come up hard and try to work their way into the screen wall, being ready to break up the pass or make the tackle. Figure 4-12 shows the inside linebackers playing the screen up the middle.

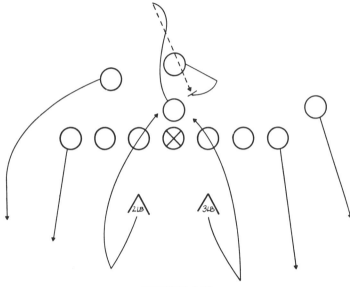

FIGURE 4-12

Play of the Safety Men in Zone Pass Defense

The three safety men (left, right, and middle safety) have the responsibility of covering the deepest receivers sent out by the offense. Each safety is to cover ⅓ of the width of the field. In case two deep receivers are sent into the ⅓ zone of a safety man, the safety should, in every case, stay with the *deeper* of the two. The cardinal sin of any safety is to let a receiver get behind him. This should be drilled into each safety until he understands it thoroughly. When we allow any receiver to get behind a safety, we are in danger of the long touchdown pass. Figure 4-13 shows the zone responsibilities of the three safeties.

One of the biggest problems we try to guard against is the safety men coming up too soon to try to stop a running play. Some defensive backs are so anxious to make the tackle that they commit themselves too soon, come up to make a tackle, and then find, only too late, that the play-action pass is developing and that a receiver is open deep in his zone.

We feel strongly that since we never ask our three safety men to rotate right or left as the ball is put in play, we will seldom be pulled out of position creating seams in the secondary. We do insist that proper pursuit angles be taken once the ball has crossed the line of scrimmage, but until that time, the safeties are to stay in their zone. Some may feel that failure to rotate weakens the defense against the running game. We don't feel that it does, but even if it did, we prefer giving up a few extra running yards rather than allowing the long pass play.

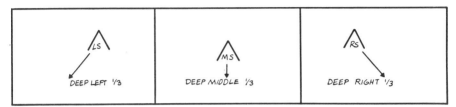

FIGURE 4-13

Each safety must learn to protect himself against having a receiver come from across the field and get behind him deep in his zone. As soon as a pass play begins to develop, each safety must scan the entire field to check for any potential receiver crossing into his zone (Figure 4-14).

Another potential danger to the safety men is the throw-back pass. If each safety is drilled *to stay in his zone until the ball has crossed the line of scrimmage,* he will seldom have the throw-back pass completed in his zone. Figure 4-15 shows the left safety protecting against the throw-back pass in his zone.

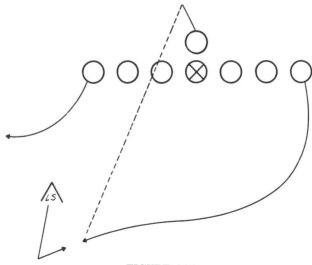

FIGURE 4-14

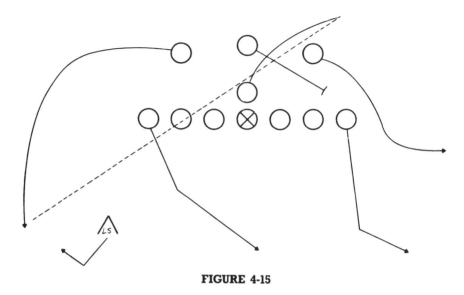

FIGURE 4-15

A good coaching point to remember is that the safety men should not get *extremely* deep just for the sake of getting deep each time a pass develops. If they do, they will find the offensive team completing medium-length passes in front of them almost at will. Each safety should use judgment on how deep to get, based on his own speed, the speed of the receivers, the game situation, and the offensive tendencies of the opponent. Each safety should strive to stay about two steps deeper than the deepest receiver in his area.

When the entire 44 Stack defense is playing zone pass defense, the seven pass defense zones will be covered as shown in Figure 4-16.

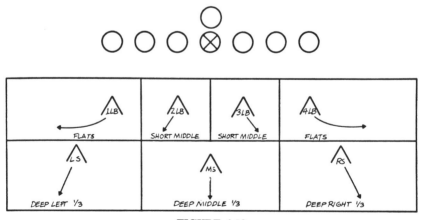

FIGURE 4-16

PLAYING THE 44 STACK MAN-TO-MAN PASS DEFENSE

There are two reasons which compelled us to play some man-to-man pass defense along with our regular zone coverage:

1. Some formations have extremely wide receivers and often two extremely wide receivers are placed on the same side of the offense. This makes zone coverage very difficult as it places a burden on one of the safety men.

2. Some opponents have receivers who are not as fast as our defensive backs. We feel that we can move up closer to the line of scrimmage, and by keying their moves, more easily read whether the play is to be a pass or a run.

As a general rule, when playing a man-to-man defense, we assign the widest eligible receiver on our left to our left safety. The second widest eligible receiver to our left is assigned to the Unit 1 linebacker. We do the same with the right side of our defense by giving our right safety the responsibility for picking up the widest receiver to our right with the Unit 4 linebacker taking the second widest receiver. The Unit 2 and Unit 3 linebackers key the fullback. The Unit 2 linebacker takes the fullback if he releases for a pass to our left. The Unit 3 linebacker goes with the fullback if he releases to our right. We also have the benefit of having a free safety who is our middle safety man. Figures 4-17 to 4-20 show our normal man-to-man coverage against four different formations.

When facing the I-formation, we have found it best to cover eligible receivers as shown in Figure 4-21. We no longer have a free safety, but we are better prepared to cover the tailback if he releases for a pass. The

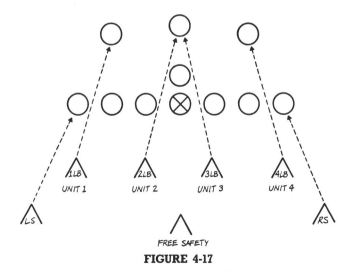

FIGURE 4-17

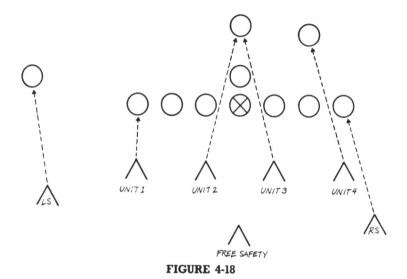

FIGURE 4-18

Unit 1 and Unit 4 linebackers both key the tailback. If he releases for a pass to our left, the Unit 1 linebacker takes him. If he releases to our right the Unit 4 linebacker covers him.

In teaching the man-to-man coverage, we tell our three safeties to get slightly closer to the line of scrimmage. Since they already know who they are to cover they can afford to get a little nearer. Also they can come up quicker on a running play.

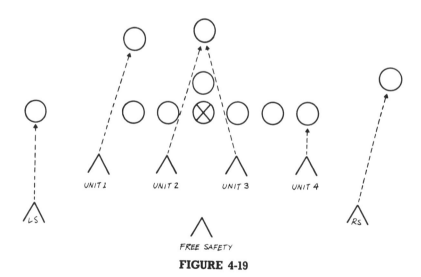

FIGURE 4-19

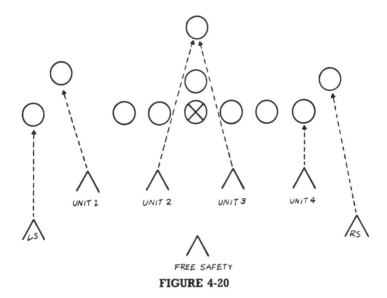

FIGURE 4-20

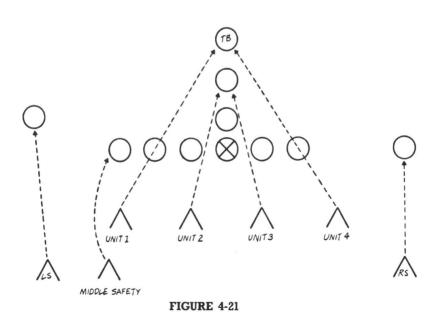

FIGURE 4-21

The Automatic Man-to-Man

Most formations are balanced in that they have two eligible receivers on the left side and two eligible receivers on the right side with a fullback in the middle. When defensing a formation of this type, we use our outside safety men and outside linebackers to cover the two receivers on either side and still have the luxury of a free safety. However, when the offense lines up or shifts into a formation that has *three* eligible receivers on one side, we change to our automatic man-to-man coverage. This gives our free safety a man-to-man assignment on the three-receiver side.

Figure 4-22 shows a formation with three eligible receivers to our left. We assign the widest receiver to our left safety. The second widest receiver is now given to the middle safety (formerly free safety) with the third widest receiver being taken by the Unit 1 linebacker. Notice the change from the regular man-to-man in that we assign the second widest receiver to the middle safety instead of to the Unit 1 linebacker. We do this because we feel that the second receiver can release downfield faster than the player in the third receiver position. The middle safety is aligned deeper to begin with; therefore, he is in better position to cover the second receiver.

We change to the automatic man-to-man coverage anytime an offense shows three receivers lined up to one side. If we didn't change to the automatic man-to-man coverage, the offense could send three receivers to the left (or right) side of our defense with only two pass

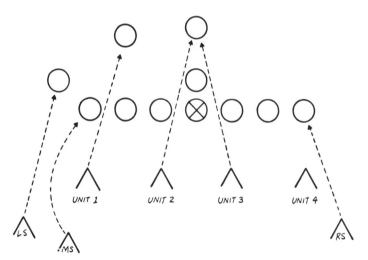

FIGURE 4-22

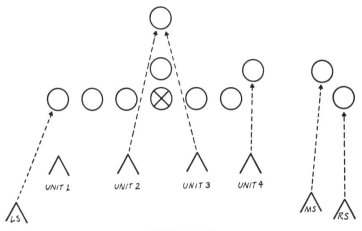

FIGURE 4-23

defenders in the immediate area. The defensive team must be drilled to recognize any offense that contains three receivers on one side and to call out "automatic left (or right)" so that all pass defenders can pick up their proper man. Figures 4-23 and 4-24 show offenses containing three eligible receivers on one side, and the adjustments that should be made by using the automatic man-to-man coverage.

The Match-Up Man-to-Man

When playing man-to-man defense, we have sometimes found it to our benefit to shift one or two of our pass defenders around to help them

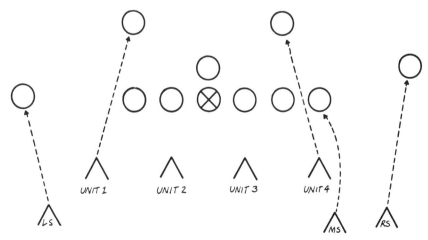

FIGURE 4-24

better match up with certain offensive personnel. We do not like to do this unless we feel certain a serious mismatch could occur with our defender getting the worst of it.

Let's say the offense has an extremely fast flanker who always lines up to our left side. If our left safety isn't our fastest defensive back, we could get hurt quickly by the mismatch in speed. Therefore, we should move our middle or right safety man (whoever is faster) to our left side and match him up with their fastest receiver. Or we may need to move another of our defenders to match up with an offensive end who stands 6′5″ tall.

When using the match-up man-to-man against the flip-flop offense, the pass defenders should remain in the middle of the defense until the offense breaks the huddle. Then each defender can easily go right or left to match up with the receiver he is to cover (Figure 4-25).

Inside Linebackers Covering for Outside Linebackers on Man-to-Man Pass Defense

Sometimes we desire to play man-to-man pass defense, yet allow the outside linebacker to be free to stunt. We do this by letting the inside linebacker take the receiver normally covered by the outside linebacker.

Figure 4-26 shows man-to-man coverage vs. a full house backfield. The Unit 1 linebacker usually covers the halfback on his side in this formation. However, we have called for Unit 1 to "X" stunt. We now ask the Unit 2 linebacker to pick up the halfback for the Unit 1 linebacker. Normally, the Unit 2 and Unit 3 linebackers would *both* be covering the

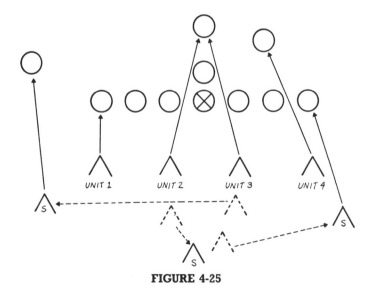

FIGURE 4-25

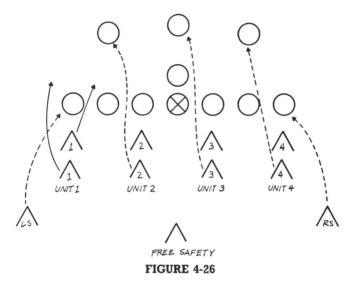

FIGURE 4-26

fullback, but now the Unit 3 linebacker covers him by himself. Good communication is a must here to insure that each receiver is properly covered.

Figure 4-27 shows an offense with a strong set to our right. We must go to the automatic man-to-man since there are three eligible receivers to our right side. This calls for our right safety to cover their wingback, our middle safety to cover their left end, and, normally, our Unit 4 linebacker would take the halfback. Again, we have called a stunt (Unit 4 "X"), so the Unit 4 linebacker instructs the Unit 3 linebacker to pick up the halfback for him. This frees the Unit 4 linebacker to proceed with his stunt. The Unit 2 linebacker covers the fullback by himself.

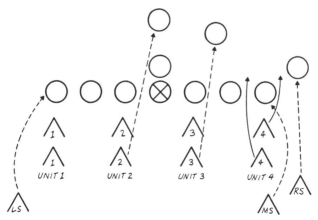

FIGURE 4-27

MAN-TO-MAN COVERAGE VERSUS MAN IN MOTION

It is imperative that any back sent in motion be covered properly if a defense is to be sound. A great deal of practice time should be spent in learning to defense the man in motion, so that when motion shows in a game, there is no hesitation on the coverage.

Once again, we state the value of a good scouting report in preparing to cover motion. Knowing which back usually goes in motion and knowing the formations of an opponent can make the job of covering a man in motion much easier for a safety or a linebacker.

We believe in keeping coverage rules as simple as possible. To require a linebacker or safety to memorize many different rules for covering motion would be difficult since there are simply too many different formations and too many positions from which motion can be sent.

There are three basic offensive patterns to consider in covering motion: (1) the *balanced* offense with two eligible receivers on each side of the center plus a fullback in the middle, (2) the *I-formation* offensive team, and (3) the *flood,* or *strong set* offense where three eligible receivers are on the same side of the center.

If the offense is *balanced,* and we are playing man-to-man defense, we cover the two receivers on each side with an outside safety man and an outside linebacker. This gives us a free middle safety man. *This free safety is given the responsibility of picking up the player who goes in motion.* This relieves all other defenders from having responsibility for covering a motion man.

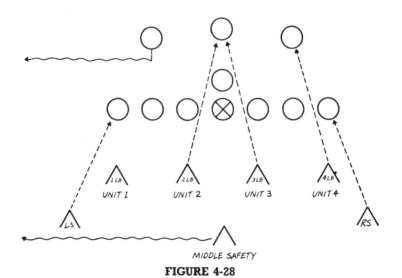

FIGURE 4-28

Figure 4-28 shows an offense with two tight ends and a full house backfield. Using normal man-to-man coverage, the Unit 1 linebacker would cover the halfback on his side. But when the halfback goes in motion, he becomes the property of the middle (free) safety, who moves down the line of scrimmage with the motion man. The Unit 1 linebacker is now free of man-to-man coverage and concentrates entirely on watching for the running play to his side.

Figure 4-29 shows a wing-T offense with the wingback going in motion. The wingback, initially, had been covered by the right safety, but as soon as motion starts, he belongs to the middle safety. The right safety, now free of man-to-man coverage, watches the play develop and is ready to help out if a run or pass develops to his side.

Figure 4-30 shows a Pro-I formation. Our right safety is covering the split end, our left safety has the flanker, and the middle safety now covers the tight end. The Unit 1 and Unit 4 linebackers both key the tailback with the Unit 2 and Unit 3 linebackers keying the fullback. If the tailback starts in motion to our right, the Unit 4 linebacker goes with him. If he goes to our left the Unit 1 linebacker has him (Figure 4-30).

Figure 4-31 illustrates another I-formation set, the Power-I. The left safety has the tight end, the middle safety covers the halfback, with the right safety on the split end. Again, the Unit 1 linebacker and the Unit 4 linebacker key the tailback and in the illustration the Unit 4 linebacker covers him since the tailback starts to our right. If the halfback had gone in motion, the middle safety would have gone with him. If the fullback had started in motion, the Unit 2 or Unit 3 linebacker would have taken him, according to the direction the fullback started in.

When the offense lines up in the *flood* or *strong set* formation, we go to the automatic man-to-man coverage as described earlier in this

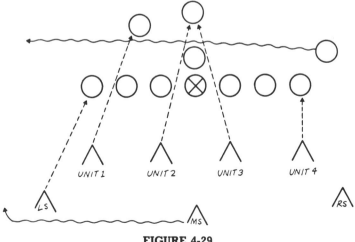

FIGURE 4-29

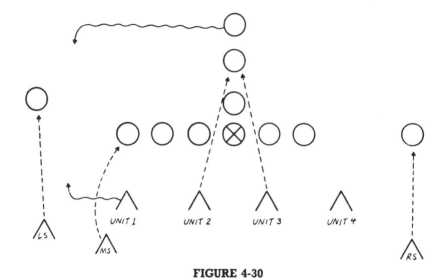

FIGURE 4-30

chapter. Now when a back goes in motion *in the same direction* as the strong set, the regular defender assigned to that back goes with him (Figures 4-32 and 4-33). However, if a back goes in motion *away* from the strong set, he is picked up by the outside linebacker on the side away from the strong set (Figures 4-34 and 4-35). The outside linebacker away from the strong set will always be free to pick up motion, since there will never be a second eligible receiver lined up on his side of the offense.

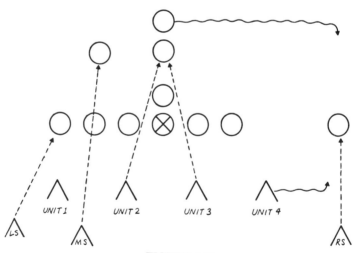

FIGURE 4-31

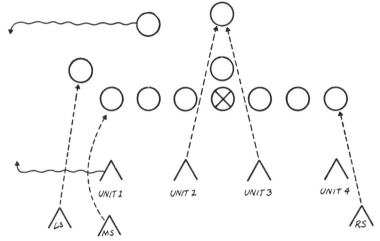

FIGURE 4-32

PASS DEFENSE VERSUS THE ROLL-OUT OR SPRINT-OUT PASS

A roll-out or sprint-out pass is one in which the quarterback moves laterally to his right or left, often going beyond the off-tackle area, at a depth of 3 to 7 yards. This type of play is very dangerous, for the threat of a fake pass and run is ever present.

When the roll or sprint-out pass begins to develop, each safety covers his ⅓ deep zone and each outside linebacker moves to his flat zone area. However, because of the constant danger of the run, one of the inside linebackers should always put pressure on the quarterback.

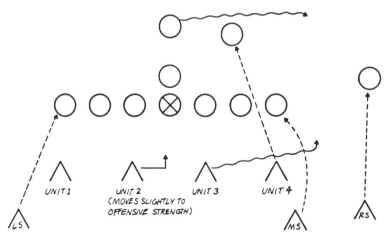

FIGURE 4-33

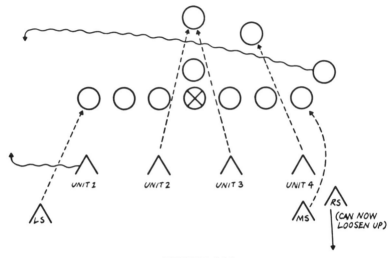

FIGURE 4-34

Figure 4-36 shows the Unit 2 inside linebacker *scraping off* to put pressure on the quarterback. As soon as the Unit 2 linebacker "reads" a roll or sprint-out pass to his side, he should move outside and up towards the quarterback, striving to keep the quarterback from getting outside him for a possible run. Notice in Figure 4-37 that the Unit 3 linebacker now covers the middle short zone by himself since the Unit 2 linebacker is pressuring the quarterback.

The linebacker who is scraping off must be coached not to cross the line of scrimmage too quickly for he may be caught inside and end up trailing the play instead of containing the quarterback (Figure 4-38).

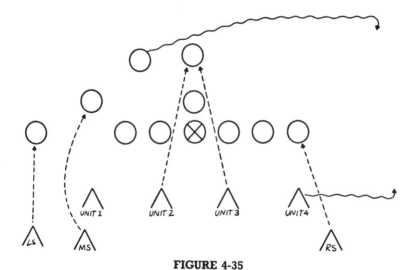

FIGURE 4-35

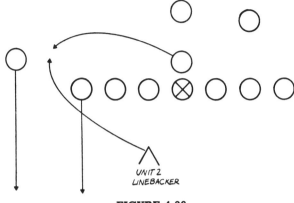

FIGURE 4-36

When facing a team that runs the roll or sprint-out play often, the inside linebackers might wish to do less stunting, so that the scrape-off can be used if needed.

THE PREVENT DEFENSE

The 44 Stack Prevent defense is used on two occasions: (1) when it is within two minutes of the half and we want to *make sure* the offense doesn't score before time runs out, and (2) at the end of the game when we are ahead and can afford to give up yardage, but must stop the touchdown.

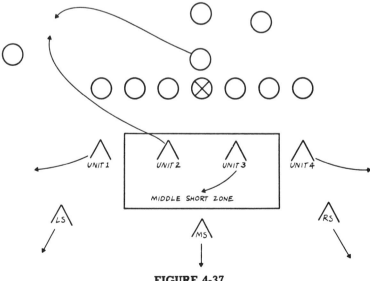

FIGURE 4-37

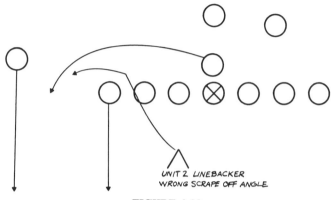

UNIT 2 LINEBACKER
WRONG SCRAPE OFF ANGLE

FIGURE 4-38

Figure 4-39 shows our prevent defense.

The front four are to rush hard, not letting the ball get outside of them. They should put pressure on the passer.

Three of the linebackers should align as shown in the illustration. They should be 3–4 yards off the line and should watch the flats and middle area for the pass. They must be especially careful of the screen or draw play.

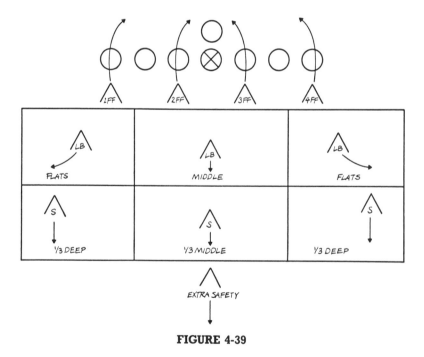

FIGURE 4-39

The three safety men should line up at least 12–15 yards deep and cover their ⅓ of the field zone. They can afford to give up a pass in front of them if necessary, but, as always, should never let a man get behind them.

The *extra safety man* should be the fastest player on the defense. He may be a linebacker or a safety. He should be a sure tackler and a dependable player with poise and plenty of determination, since he is the last man between the offense and the goal line. He should station himself 7 to 10 yards behind the regular safety. When the play starts, he should move with the flow of the ball, keeping the entire offense in front of him. This extra safety should *not* come up quickly to make a tackle, but should be a preventive measure in case the ballcarrier breaks clear of the other defenders and appears headed for a touchdown.

PERSONNEL ADJUSTMENTS FOR THE 44 STACK PASS DEFENSE

There are occasions when we feel certain that our opponent will consider throwing a pass: (1) if they are normally a strong passing team that relies on the pass to win and that will pass "anywhere or anytime," (2) if it is 2nd down and 10 or more yards to go for a first down or 3rd and 8 or more yards to go, and (3) if a team is behind and must play "catch up" in order to get back in the game.

When a likely passing situation is developing, we often insert special pass defenders into the lineup to replace any linebacker (or in some cases a safety) who, although an otherwise fine defensive player, might be a step too slow or not quite agile enough to play top-flight pass defense. For example, let's say both of our inside linebackers are big, tough players who perform well against the run and only fair against the pass. We can insert two smaller, but more agile backs into the inside linebacker positions to play pass defense, thus getting more speed into the lineup and giving us two "pass defense specialists" in the game. Since we do this only in special long-yardage situations, we seldom have to worry about the offense running right at these smaller linebackers.

5

Adjusting the 44 Stack to Different Offensive Sets

In considering adjustments to offensive sets, there are two points to remember: (1) a defense cannot remain sound unless proper adjustments can be made, and (2) the adjustments must be taught thoroughly so that the defensive players will understand when and how to adjust.

There are certain basic sets that every defense will probably face during the course of a season. These include the split end set, the wingback set, the slotback set, the strong set, the shotgun set, the unbalanced set, and the punt formation set. Although the defense may be challenged with offensive sets other than these, you and your players should be able to adapt based on the ideas presented in this chapter.

ADJUSTING TO THE SPLIT END

Some teams will split an end to enable him to more easily release downfield for a pass. Other teams may attempt to hide a weak player by placing him at split end with no intention of ever throwing to him. In either case, the defense must adjust to the split end.

The first step in adjusting to the split end is made by the outside front four man on the split end side. When the front four player sees the

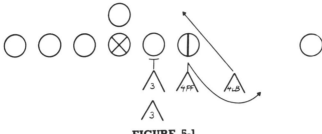

FIGURE 5-1

split end on his side, he should move to either of two positions: (1) *head-on* the offensive tackle, or (2) *outside shoulder* of the offensive tackle.

From the *head-on* position the outside front four man can play Basic or can carry out many of his normal stunts such as *Gap Out, Loop,* or *Crash.* Figure 5-1 illustrates a Crash Right stunt run to the split end side with the front four defender starting from the head-on position.

Figure 5-2 shows the split end again to our right side, with the front four player aligned on the *outside shoulder* of the offensive tackle. If not stunting, the front four player drives through the outside shoulder of the tackle. This outside shoulder alignment makes it difficult for the tackle to block the defender to the inside. It also gives the front four man a good position from which to start a pass rush and provides good outside coverage against the run. *Pass Rush to the Split End, Gap Out, Loop,* and *Slant In* are examples of stunts which can be run effectively from the outside shoulder position.

The next adjustment to a split end is made by the outside linebacker on the split end side. This defensive player can align himself in any of three positions: (1) normal, (2) walkaway, or (3) head-on the split end.

The *normal* position is shown in Figure 5-3. When playing normal the outside linebacker simply stays in the same position that he would be in if the offensive end and front four player in front of him were in their regular positions. The normal position should be used when the threat of the run is greater than the threat of the pass. It also enables the outside linebacker to stunt. Of course, the outside linebacker will not always stunt, but the offense must always consider that possibility. The normal

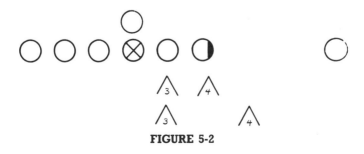

FIGURE 5-2

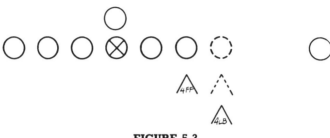

FIGURE 5-3

position allows the linebacker to retreat to his pass defense zone as usual, if a pass play develops.

The second position that can be used by the outside linebacker on the split end side is the *walkaway* position, as shown in Figure 5-4. This places the outside linebacker about halfway between the split end and the tackle and a little deeper than usual. From the walkaway position the threat of a stunt is gone, but it is a good position from which to cover the outside running plays. It also takes away the threat of the quick "look-in" pass from the quarterback to the split end (Figure 5-5), and enables the outside linebacker to move rapidly to his pass defense zone.

We like to wait until just before the snap of the ball to move to the walkaway position. This usually prevents the quarterback from having time to change the play if a "look-in" pass has been called, and also allows us to threaten the offensive team with a possible stunt and perhaps confuse their blocking plans.

When the split end is a dangerous receiver and the threat of the pass is greater than the threat of the run, the outside linebacker may choose the *head-on the split end* position (Figure 5-6). Although we use the name *head-on*, we actually prefer the outside linebacker to line up more to the inside shoulder of the split end. This forces the split end to release to the outside and generally makes the quarterback have to throw a longer pass. The longer the pass is in the air, the longer the defensive secondary has to react to the ball.

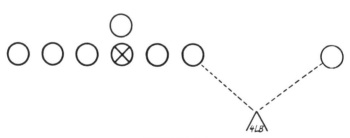

FIGURE 5-4

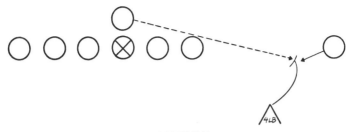

FIGURE 5-5

As soon as the ball is snapped, the outside linebacker should step towards the split end driving both hands into the shoulder pads, in a manner similar to a hand shiver. The defender should make contact several times in the first four or five yards in an attempt to delay and confuse the pass route of the split end. The outside linebacker should stay with the split end until the end has left the linebacker's pass defense zone.

When the outside linebacker is in the *head-on the split end* position, and an offensive halfback is on the split end side, we often allow the inside linebacker on that side to get wider, as shown in Figure 5-7. The inside linebacker is now in better position to help out in the wide area between the tackle and the split end, yet is still in position to stunt with his front four partner.

ADJUSTING TO THE WINGBACK

The wingback can be a very effective weapon because he can be utilized as a blocker, pass receiver, ballcarrier, or man-in-motion. There are two ways we have successfully adjusted to the wingback. Figure 5-8 shows our outside linebacker moving to a position directly opposite the wingback. The outside linebacker should key the wingback to determine whether the play is a pass or a run. If the wingback steps towards the linebacker, the linebacker must meet his charge with force and not allow himself to be blocked in or out. When using this adjustment, the outside linebacker is still in position to carry out most of his stunts.

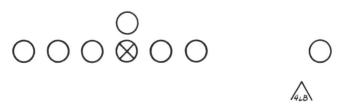

FIGURE 5-6

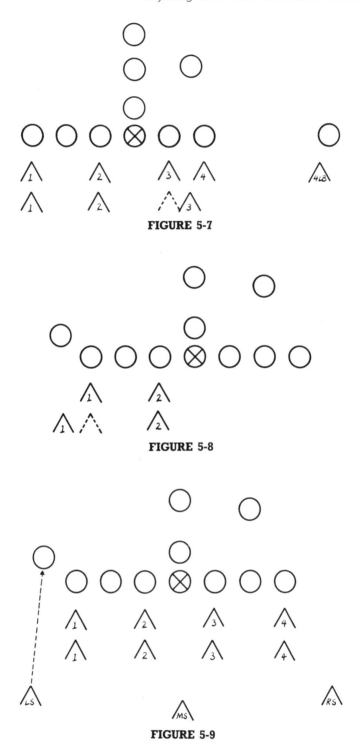

FIGURE 5-7

FIGURE 5-8

FIGURE 5-9

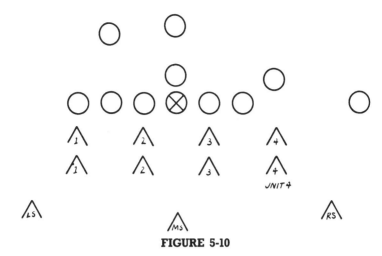

FIGURE 5-10

The other adjustment to the wingback offense is to align in the man-to-man defense as shown in Figure 5-9. This allows our four units to play the normal 44 Stack defense and brings the outside safety to a position where he keys the wingback. If the wingback blocks, the outside safety comes up fast to the outside to protect against the run. If the wingback releases, the outside safety covers him man-to-man. This adjustment allows us to continue with full stunts by all units.

ADJUSTING TO THE SLOTBACK

There are several variations of the slotback offense. Figure 5-10 shows a formation where the offense has split an end and positioned the slotback about where a normal tight end would play (the slotback is a yard off the line of scrimmage, of course). This presents no problem as our Unit 4 defenders can line up directly opposite the slotback in exactly the same position that they would be in if they were facing a normal tight end.

Figure 5-11 shows the slotback stationed four or five yards from the tackle. As long as the slotback is no wider than this, the outside linebacker should move directly in front of him. The linebacker should key the moves of the slotback and be ready to help out on a run to his side or cover his zone if a pass play develops.

Figure 5-12 illustrates a tight slot formation with the tackle, end, and slotback no more than normal line splits apart. We adjust to the tight slot in the same manner in which we adjusted to a wingback. In Figure 5-12 our Unit 1 front four man is head-on the slotback and the Unit 1 linebacker has moved directly across from the tight end.

The defense can also adjust by calling man-to-man coverage as shown in Figure 5-13.

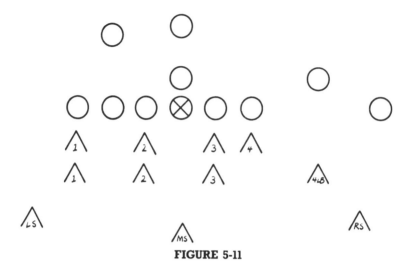

FIGURE 5-11

ADJUSTING TO THE SHOTGUN SPREAD

When facing a shotgun spread formation, we usually find three eligible receivers on one side of the quarterback and two eligible receivers on the other side. Since there are three receivers on one side, the defenders should automatically use man-to-man coverage as shown in Figure 5-14. This coverage requires the middle safety to play man-to-man instead of being a free safety, but allows the front four players and linebackers to execute any desired stunt.

If you feel that the threat of a pass from the shotgun is much greater than the threat of a run, you may wish to adjust as shown in Figure 5-15.

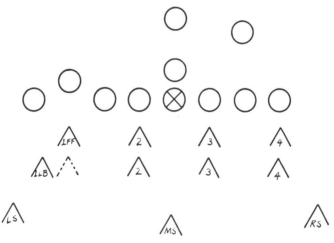

FIGURE 5-12

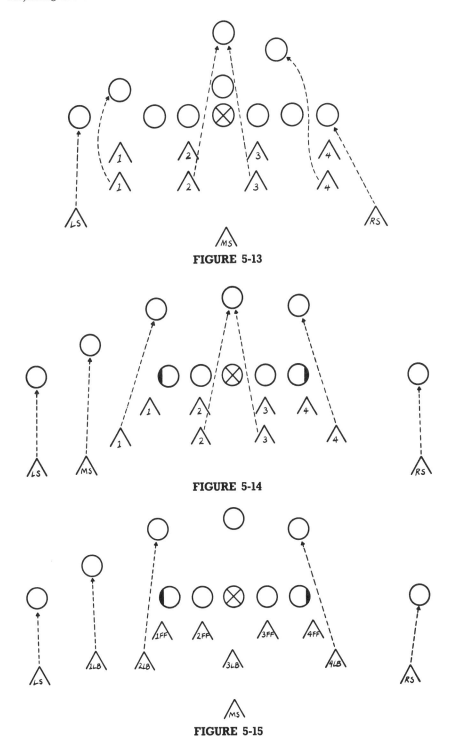

FIGURE 5-13

FIGURE 5-14

FIGURE 5-15

The defense has now shifted the linebackers towards the three-receiver side of the offense. The middle safety plays as a free safety. The other receivers are covered man-to-man as follows: left safety covers widest receiver on his side, Unit 1 linebacker takes second widest receiver, Unit 2 linebacker covers the third widest receiver, Unit 4 linebacker picks up the second widest receiver on his side, and the right safety covers the widest receiver to his side. This adjustment eliminates most stunt possibilities, but does provide excellent pass coverage against the shotgun offense.

ADJUSTING TO THE STRONG SET

Figure 5-16 shows a strong offensive set to our left side. The defense has adjusted to the automatic man-to-man coverage as explained in Chapter 4, and any of the four units can stunt as usual.

In Figure 5-17, the defense has adjusted to the strong set by shifting all linebackers towards the strong set side and playing a zone pass defense. Most stunts can still be utilized from this alignment.

You should decide which of these two adjustments would be most beneficial considering the play tendencies of the offensive team.

ADJUSTING TO THE PUNT FORMATION

Figure 5-18 illustrates our adjustment to a normal punt formation. There are three safety men in position to handle the punt. One is located in the short middle area, directly over the center, and about 20 to 25 yards deep. His job is to fair catch a short punt. He also is responsible for clearing his teammates away from a short punt, so that the ball will not accidentally hit one of them.

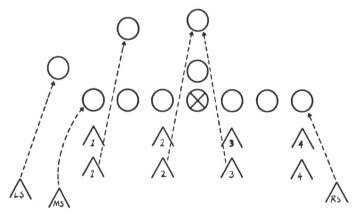

FIGURE 5-16

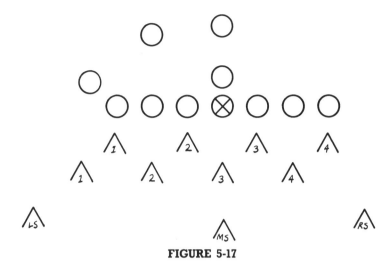

FIGURE 5-17

The other two safety men are in position to handle the punt if it is kicked deep. The depth of these two men will vary according to the ability of the punter to get distance in his kicks. One of the deep receivers should call for the punt as soon as it is possible to determine who can best handle it. The other receiver should stay about 5 or 6 yards away to check for a fumble or to serve as a blocker for the one who catches the punt.

Other than the three safety men, the remaining defenders align in their normal 44 Stack positions.

From this punt formation alignment, the defensive team can make one of three decisions: (1) rush the punter, (2) delay the offensive linemen at the line of scrimmage, or (3) set up a return.

To rush the punter, we call *All Units "X"* (Figure 5-19). This provides us with an eight-man rush. The defenders in Unit 1 and Unit 4 who are rushing from the outside should be careful to keep an outside position on the punter so that he will not fake a kick and run around end. If the punting team has been known to fake the punt and pass to an end or back, one of the Units 1 and 4 defenders should drop back a few yards off the line of scrimmage as the ball is snapped to protect against this type of play.

When the punter is not consistent in getting good distance in his kicks, we often call for our defenders to delay the offensive linemen at the line of scrimmage. This usually gives our safety men ample time to field the short punt. We delay the offensive linemen as shown in Figure 5-20. The Units 1 and 4 front four men are assigned to the tight ends, the Units 2 and 3 front four men are assigned to the offensive guards, and the Units 2 and 3 linebackers are responsible for delaying the tackles from getting downfield rapidly. The safety in the short middle area delays the center.

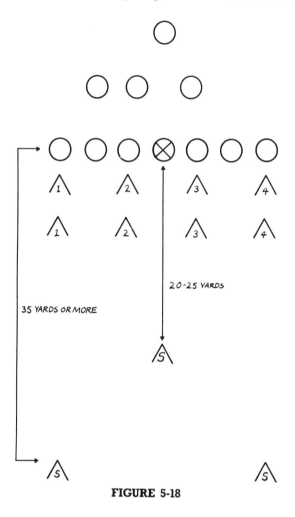

FIGURE 5-18

On the snap of the ball, each of these defenders steps in front of his assigned offensive lineman and "blocks" him in much the same manner as he would block for his own punter. The defender must attempt to remain with his lineman as long as possible. As the lineman begins to free himself from the "block" and release downfield, the defender should go with him and continue to block him. The defender must be careful not to let the offensive lineman turn his back in such a manner as to create the possibility of a clip. The outside linebackers are not given a specific "delaying" assignment, but should watch for a run or pass, then pick up any player not being blocked.

Figure 5-21 shows our punt return procedure which is equally

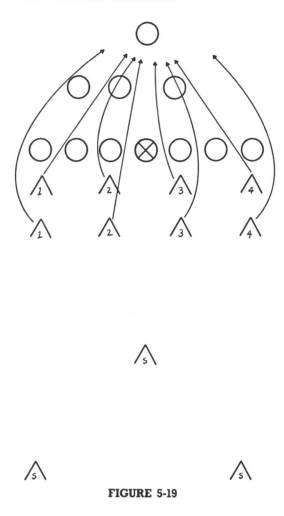

FIGURE 5-19

effective to either side of the field. As one deep receiver handles the punt, the other deep receiver should direct him right or left, then lead him behind the wall of four blockers. *Coaching point:* Notice that the Unit 1 front four man and the Unit 4 linebacker will rush the punter before taking their places in the wall. This gives us a check against the bad snap from center over the punter's head, as well as discouraging the punter from considering a fake punt and run.

If the defensive team faces a type of punt formation that positions a player wide to the outside (Figure 5-22), we move an outside linebacker to a walkaway position. This is to guard against a quick pass resulting in a first down or a long gainer.

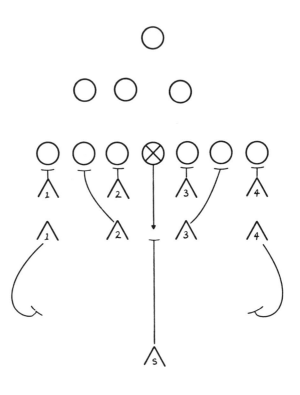

FIGURE 5-20

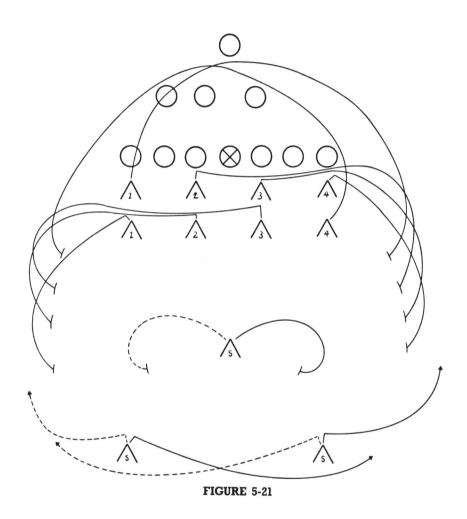

FIGURE 5-21

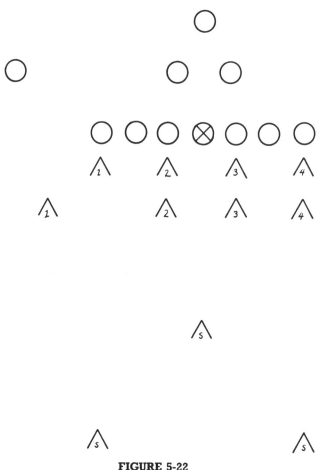

FIGURE 5-22

ADJUSTING TO THE UNBALANCED LINE

In adjusting to an unbalanced line we cover every other offensive lineman with a front four defender as usual (this places a front four man head-on the center). We then adjust (if necessary) the linebackers according to the positioning of the offensive backs. In Figure 5-23, the offensive backs are strong to the defensive right. Therefore, we move our linebackers to our right giving the defense more balance with the offense.

Even though there are many backfield alignments that can be combined with an unbalanced line, the defenders need only remember to keep the front four playing as usual, and slide the linebackers right or left to match strength with the offensive backs.

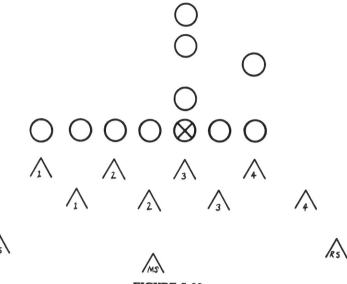

FIGURE 5-23

6

The Rover 44 Adjustment

For years we used the straight 44 Stack defense with great success, but we continued to look for ways to improve it. Recently we came up with our version of the Rover 44 Adjustment, which immediately seemed to make our defense 50 percent stronger and even more flexible than before.

When an opponent splits an end, they have only two blockers (guard and tackle) to one side while we have four defenders (tackle, end, one inside linebacker, and one outside linebacker). (Figure 6-1.)

We decided that one of these men could be used elsewhere to strengthen another defensive area. (We would still have three defenders against two blockers on the split end side.) The inside linebacker (2 or 3 LB) on the split end side is designated to be our *Rover*.

There are five Rover calls:

- Rover Fire
- Rover Soft
- Rover Tackle
- Rover Center
- Rover Man-to-Man

When a Rover call is made, the inside linebacker on the split end side goes to his newly assigned area adding greater strength to that area. Here's how it works:

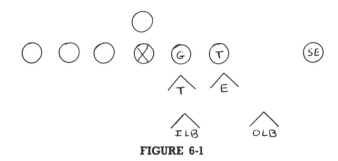

FIGURE 6-1

ROVER FIRE: This call places our Rover on the tight end side and fires him into the backfield (Figure 6-2).

This call is good against a team that likes to run to the tight end side. It gives the appearance of a five-man line, which in fact it is. This call helps stop sweeps, options, and off-tackle plays. It is a good call against a team that uses a wingback (put Rover on the wingback side). Use the Rover Fire call in connection with all other stunts. Example: *Rover Fire, All Gap In.*

ROVER SOFT: This call is similar to the Rover Fire call, but we want the Rover to "play soft" and not immediately attack the offense (Figure 6-3). The Rover lines up on the tight end side and plays along the line of scrimmage. He can be effective in stringing out a wide sweep or covering a pitch man on an option play. This is also a good call against a team that screens to the tight end side. Use this call in connection with all other stunts.

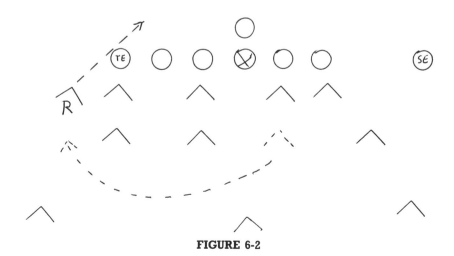

FIGURE 6-2

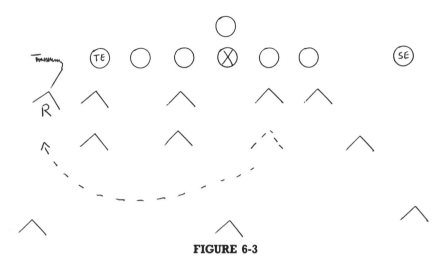

FIGURE 6-3

ROVER TACKLE: The Rover lines up head-on the offensive tackle on the tight end side (Figure 6-4). This adds strength against a running play to the tight end side. It provides three down linemen and two linebackers opposite an offensive end, tackle, and guard. The Rover Tackle can be instructed to just play *Basic* or to *Gap In/Out* (left or right). This call can be made with all other stunts. Example: *Rover Tackle, Crash to TE side.*

Coaching point: A substitute defensive tackle could be sent in to replace the linebacker when this call is made if a "larger, front-line type" of player is desired.

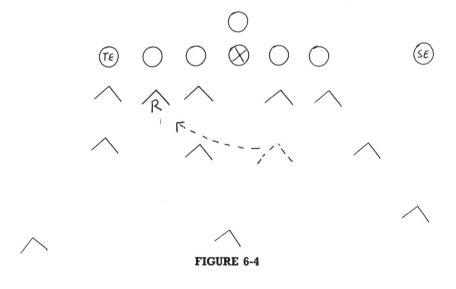

FIGURE 6-4

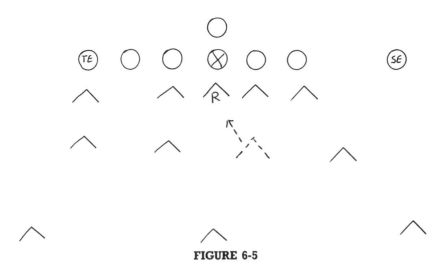

FIGURE 6-5

ROVER CENTER: The Rover lines up head-on the offensive center (Figure 6-5). He can play *Basic* (much like a middle guard in the 5-2 defense) or can *Gap Left or Right*. The Rover Center call can help stop the trap play up the middle as well as fullback dive plays. This is also a good short-yardage call.

Coaching point: A substitute defensive lineman can replace the inside linebacker when this call is made, providing a "larger" player on the front line.

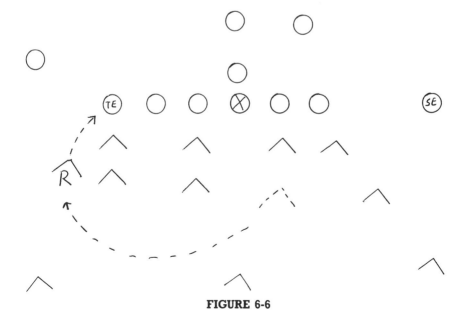

FIGURE 6-6

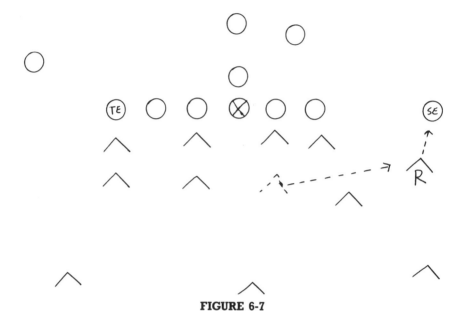

FIGURE 6-7

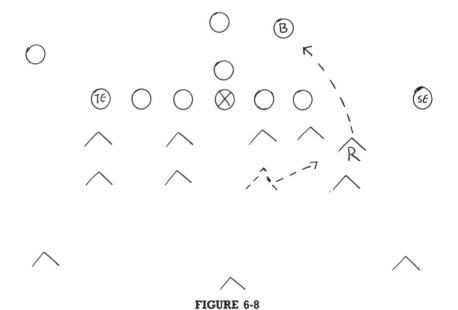

FIGURE 6-8

ROVER MAN-TO-MAN: This is a pass defense call that can really stop a pass offense that features one great receiver. Find the receiver who is hurting you the most—the tight end, a wide receiver, or even a back coming out of the backfield. Assign the Rover to him for man-to-man coverage. *Important*: All other linebackers and safety men (cornerbacks and safety) play *zone* coverage as described in Chapter 4. The Rover lines up covering the good receiver as shown in Figures 6-6, 6-7, and 6-8, and stays with him in man-to-man coverage all over the field.

Coaching point: You may want to replace the Rover linebacker with a substitute defensive back who may do a better job of playing pass defense.

The flexibility that the five Rover calls add to our defense is amazing. We feel that with intelligent calls we can adequately cover any offensive situation.

7

The 45 Adjustment

This special adjustment has worked wonders for our defense. It is so simple it can be installed in a matter of minutes. The 45 Adjustment is designed as a defense against the *run* and is best used against teams that don't want to throw or can't throw effectively.

To create the 45 Adjustment, bring the middle safety up from 10 yards deep and place him directly over the center at a depth of about 4½ to 5 yards. From this position he is *not* close enough to the line of scrimmage to be immediately blocked effectively by an offensive lineman, yet he *is* close enough to fill gaps and make tackles near the line of scrimmage. He should be able to roam freely from sideline to sideline. (The 45 Adjustment is shown in Figure 7-1.) Next, place the 4 linebackers in their "Linebackers Wide" position (see Chapter 3) thereby creating room in the middle for the middle safety (now a fifth linebacker). Finally, drop the left and right safety men (cornerbacks) back several yards with instructions to cover *one-half* of the field *deep*.

Use every stunt in the 44 Stack defense and still have the luxury of having an extra, or "backup," linebacker in the middle. One of the best stunt calls from the 45 is *1 and 4 Gap In, 2 and 3 Gap Out*. This call gives excellent, and safe, outside coverage, off-tackle coverage, and up-the-middle coverage against the run (Figure 7-2).

The *45 Defense with all X* is a good call that allows eight players to attack with a backup linebacker in the middle (Figure 7-3).

Obviously, a potential weakness in the 45 is having only two players to cover the deep pass. So remember to make the 45 call:

1. against run-oriented teams

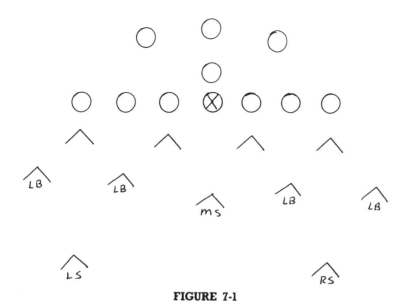

FIGURE 7-1

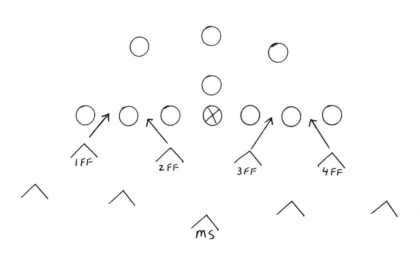

FIGURE 7-2

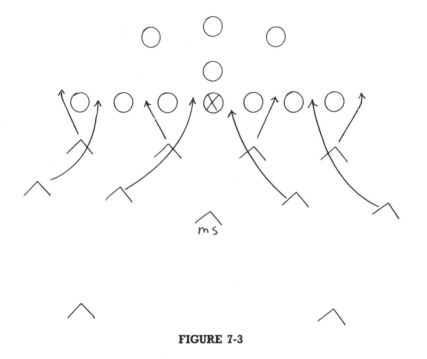

FIGURE 7-3

2. when it is obviously a "running" down (such as 3rd down and 2
   yards to go)

3. when it is obvious you will get beat unless you stop the powerful
   running attack of your opponent.

If the offense *does* pass when you are in the 45 you still have the four
linebackers going to their short zones, two deep backs covering deep one-
half each, plus the middle safety (fifth linebacker) retreating quickly to
his middle zone. Or, of course, you can easily use man-to-man coverage
from the 45 (see Chapter 4 on pass defense).

Remember, the 45 is most effective when used with the wide variety
of stunts available to the 44 Stack defense.